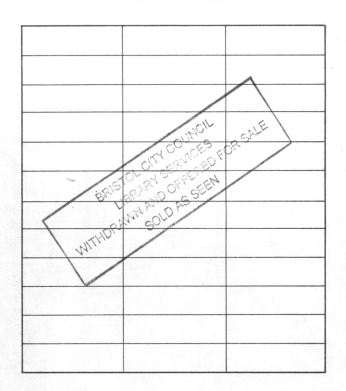

In a book entitled *Wheels*, inevitably there is a preponderance
of photographs of locomotives. Equal... ... ... of
railway, region, time, ... of
photographs, other tha...
abundance and difficul... ... ... e.
Spanning the gap betwe... ... ... or
Barton Wright, Kirtley... ... ... or
the final flowering of ste... ... ... or Bulleid,
stands *Sir Gilbert Claughton* himself (herself?): No 2222
appropriately enters Crewe station on 2 March 1913. The
'Claughton' had especially large wheel-centres. How I wish it
had been my camera! That magnificent signal gantry reminds
... ... working practice
... the 'Premier Line', but
... ys. This was a 'real'
... pride and precision, and
... – such as that last LNWR
... MS No 5101), just visible
... scene never to be
... orld.

WHEELS

ROBERT ADLEY
WHEELS

LONDON
IAN ALLAN LTD

Dedication

To the Adley family for their patience, as ever, and also to Kay Dixon for her wizardry in reading my handwriting and her patience in typing the manuscript.

Acknowledgement to National Railway Museum and Science Museum

The National Railway Museum has built up an outstanding collection of archive material and railway photographs. The NRM Library fulfils a priceless role in assembling a national archive of photographs. Notwithstanding access to the excellent Ian Allan Library, I have deliberately chosen to utilise material from the NRM Library as a tribute to the dedication of the staff at the Museum. Excepting my own material, virtually all the black and white photographs in this book are from the NRM Library, to which I pay tribute and give thanks for its inestimable assistance in preparing this book; uncredited photographs are thus attributed.

My gratitude also to the staff at the Science Museum for their help in assembling and preparing the material for the coloured drawings of locomotives.

CONTENTS

Left:
**Maurice Earley's contribution to the NRM Library is
epitomised by LMS 'Jubilee' No 5568 *Western Australia* on the
up 'Thames-Forth' at Ais Gill in 1939.**

In Memoriam
At the point of completion of the publication of
this book, there took place the tragic death of
Brian Haresnape. His role in this book is clearly
recorded; may it be a memorial to a friend not
only of mine, but of countless railway enthusiasts.
Brian coined the phrase 'Brotherhood of Steam'.
To him, and to his memory — *valete*.

Wheels are made to go round. That is what I have been saying to myself every day for many years. And except when I am on holiday, or away from my work for any other reason, I am making them go round.

Beautiful big wheels they are, too. Six feet nine inches in diameter — which is taller than any man I know — I make them go round thousands of times in the course of a day. And the faster they go the better I am pleased.

My wheels are those of the locomotive that hauls the 'Royal Scot', that fine LMS Railway train that speeds along the whole length of England and part of Scotland every day.

Driver L. A. Earl
Speeding North with the 'Royal Scot'

Left:
Bulleid Firth Brown (BFB) Wheels: little did I realise, on taking this photograph of the wheels of Bulleid 'Q1' 0-6-0 No 33029 at Three Bridges shed in April 1963 that it would appear in a book nearly a quarter of a century later.

INTRODUCTION

It is eight years since last I wrote a book for Ian Allan. In contemplating the changes in railway books that have occurred in the intervening years, it is immediately apparent that the phrase 'wrote a book' is itself a misnomer for my minor deed of authorship involved in *British Steam in Cameracolour 1962-68*. All I did was to add captions — extended and carefully-researched, but nonetheless merely captions — to a selection of my own colour photographs. I wrote an Introduction, and Sir Peter Parker wrote a Foreword. It was the colour of my photographs, not their artistic merit, that convinced Ian Allan and his colleagues to gamble on publishing what became the first large format, all-colour book of British Rail working steam. Without precedent to guide either author or publisher, we merely followed the traditional style of black-and-white photographic albums, by packing the book with illustrations, and adding captions. I recall my intention to expand, in my captions, beyond the traditional, minimal factual reference to the accompanying photograph. Date, place and class were naturally essential ingredients, but I wanted to write more, to personalise and even to romanticise. Ian Allan's editorial direction was benevolent, and my method and style earned neither rebuke nor the heavy red pencil.

British Steam in Cameracolour broke new ground. All copies were sold. Colour railway books were marketable and practical. My appetite was whetted. A very few weeks after publication, a chance meeting, appropriately on a train, brought me into contact with Blandford Press. What they lacked in knowledge and experience of railway books was compensated for by boldness and resources. At their suggestion was born a new style of railway book. They sought not technical detail, specialist information or knowledgeable historic data, but reminiscence aligned to more of my photographs. After a ghastly contretemps with an editor with no railway knowledge or enthusiasm, and my insistence on their

reprinting the entire proofs as I had originally written them, there was born book number two — *In Search of Steam*. To my astonishment their intuition was crowned with success. On the basis of not changing a winning formula, we repeated the exercise — once, twice and thrice, including another first — the first book in colour devoted exclusively to steam in China.

By now, the anecdotal formula for railway books, and the use of colour photographs from the last decade or so of British working steam, were both acceptable attributes for those publishers with resources and access to material. With the growth of the Railway Book Club, and the surprisingly strong and continuing demand for illustrations of 'real' as opposed to preserved railways, has happily come to the dramatic technical improvements in colour printing technology. Printing methods entailing the ability to colour-correct individual plates rather than to equalise an entire sheet, have been an untold boon to me, merely a 'railway enthusiast with camera', rather than a 'railway photographer'; some of my compositionally ordinary and technically poor photographs have come out of the 'discard' category into the 'usable'.

With four similar books out of the Blandford stable, it is Ian Allan's turn again to ring the changes — and whether or not we succeed depends on how many others are sharing your experience of reading this Introduction. The proposition is this — that colour photographs of working British steam, although few, are now an acceptable publishing risk: that pure anecdotal narrative could now benefit by the addition of some specialisation and 'organisation', again in a manner not previously attempted. Thus perhaps the most basic element of locomotive interest, namely designation by class and wheel-arrangement, aligned to colour photographs of working steam from its declining years on British Rail, can tap another seam in an unending mine of

8

interest to which can be attributed the success of Britain's railway publishing houses.

It goes without saying that this is not a learned tome seeking to detail the development of Britain's steam locomotives from Rainhill's 0-4-0s to Riddles' 2-10-0. I have neither the knowledge, the ability nor the photographs to undertake such a gargantuan task. My very modest aim is to produce an inchoate, partial and personalised alignment of some of my remaining unpublished colour photographs, with the amateur's comments on the class and wheel-arrangement to which they belong. By the end of 1962, when my photography began in almost-earnest, many of the earlier wheel-arrangements were but a memory. Yet surprisingly, even at this twilight hour of British steam there was plenty of variety. In preparing my notes for this book, I scoured my catalogue and noted that the following wheel-arrangements had appeared before my lens between November 1962 and August 1968:

2-10-0	0-6-0	2-6-2T
2-8-0	4-4-0	0-6-2T
0-8-0	4-8-0T	0-6-0T
4-6-2	2-8-2T	0-4-4T
4-6-0	2-8-0T	0-4-2T
2-6-2	4-6-2T	2-4-0T
2-6-0	2-6-4T	0-4-0T

This book is devoted mainly to working British locomotives, but since their demise from BR's normal revenue-earning service, there have been further images of steam before my lens, in the three categories of 'foreign', 'preserved' and 'scrapped'. To the British enthusiast all three may have a place in his affection, but only to a limited degree. As a generalisation, the more modern overseas motive-power, certainly the newer postwar designs, have been either eight or ten-coupled machines, with the accent on power and acceptable axle-loading rather than on speed. Sprinters like Drummond's 'T9', or prestige engines like *The Great Bear*, are seen now to be from another era, long gone.

The spirit of experimentation with wheel-arrangements was not much manifest in the closing years of British steam; there was a world of difference in the motives that inspired, shall we say, the Great Eastern 'Decapod' of 1902, and Robin Riddles' '9F' 2-10-0. It is no mere coincidence that Riddles' '9F' precursor, his WD 'Austerity' 2-10-0, emerged in the same generation as the German 'Kriegslok' or the Russian 'FD' 2-10-2s, precursor of the Chinese 'QJ' class.

'Class': that's the word. We know full well the meaning of the word, and its use in railway terminology. Outwith our firmament however it might have different meanings. For each interpretation it has certain common images — of style, of standard, of appearance and indeed of sound. *In extremis* one might even add 'of smell'. The eye, the ear, the nose — these are the organs by which we judge class, be they of humans or of locomotives. Thank goodness, however, I am neither sociologist nor historian, for to take this analogy any deeper would get me into serious trouble. I reject utterly the use of the word 'class' to categorise my fellow citizens, but it is not only appropriate but essential to use the word to describe steam engines. This then is a book about 'class'; the sight, the sound, the smell; the triple appeal of steam. Readers of my previous books know full well my limitations. It is quite beyond my wit, knowledge or indeed desire to seek to emulate or to copy the learned authors with which our interest is so richly blessed. This is a book of images and words, rather than of artistry and science. My self-description is merely 'railway enthusiast with camera'. If music be the food of love, then photographs are the food of memory. Words are the fuel perhaps. Now is the time to set aside my shovel lest I overfill the firebox — like most politicians, I find it harder to *stop* writing than to start! Let class be determined by wheels — wheels of steam. For me 'Co-Co' sounds like a hot drink, and merits no real place juxtaposed alongside the word 'class'.

Deciding *which* wheel-arrangements merit chapters was comparatively easy, largely dependent as it is on the availability of my photographs. Deciding *what* to write was, however, a much more difficult task. There is neither merit nor objective let alone morality in trying to emulate the *cognoscenti* by plagiarism. My theme is wheels; my medium the camera; my words to enhance my illustrations must be related thereto by some factor other than the technical. What is the link between word and picture around the chosen theme of wheels? Not 'how', for that would be technical. Not just 'when' for we know the timesphere is mainly 1962-68. Not 'who' for the biographers of steam's great engineers are legion. With what are we left? 'What' indeed, and maybe 'where' as well. I ramble on — and perhaps a 'steam ramble on wheels' is as apt a description as can be found from this practitioner's photo-motivated pen.

My books, like my life, are unplanned. In spite of good intentions honestly discussed with publisher, it is usual for me to be surprised at the ultimate style and content of my books. That confession may illustrate irresolution, ignorance, or indiscipline, or yet just 'author's licence'.

It certainly accounts for the need for two distinct sections to the Introduction to this book. Only when I was well embarked on this journey did it occur to me to write — in *Wheels* — a chapter on the wheel itself. As ever it was my wife Jane who goaded me into attempting such a task. Between her admonition and my lack of engineering or mechanical knowledge looms a chasm of potential disaster. To my secretary Kay Dixon is owed an immense debt of gratitude, and not only for deciphering my scrawl and typing the book. She it was who pointed me in the direction of the Institution of Mechanical Engineers, an establishment so august as to cause me to question my credentials even to ask for help and guidance for such a book as this. Of time, of knowledge, of encouragement, they gave most generously.

To write such a book, to compile the charts, needs endless reference. I abjure a page of 'Bibliography', for so to include such references seems pretentious and incongruous. Where appropriate, reference is made in the text to books, magazines and articles from which information has been gleaned. To Dr John Coiley at the National Railway Museum and to Tony Hall-Patch at the Science Museum debts are owed and thanks are due.

This is my first book to include a substantial number of black and white photographs. A handful were taken by me on black and white film; some are black and white conversions from my colour transparencies, one of which has appeared as a colour photograph in previous books; but most have come from the collections held at York in the possession of the National Railway Museum. My thanks are particularly due to the NRM library staff, to whom I am extremely grateful for their patience and assistance.

To the Science Museum also a considerable debt of thanks is due and is duly and pleasurably acknowledged. In my last book — the name of which I foreswear not to mention lest so to do might cause annoyance to a certain reviewer! — there was included a colour reproduction, previously unpublished, of a working drawing of an 0-6-0 from a class designed by Holmes for the North British Railway in 1888 and built by Sharp Stewart in 1892 in Glasgow. A large quantity of the working drawings was purchased by the Science Museum from the North British Locomotive Company (NBL) in 1962. The collection includes locomotives built by Dubs, Neilson, Neilson Reid, Sharp Stewart — all eventually encompassed within the NBL empire. Locomotives destined for the four corners of the earth were built here, and included some weird and wonderful machines such as a 4-10-2T for China in 1900. For this book, therefore, I returned to Tony Hall-Patch at the Science Museum for more of these drawings, which seem most appropriate in a book entitled *Wheels* and dealing with wheel-arrangements. He put me in touch with David Bryden, formerly Assistant Keeper of the Pictorial Archive Collection, whose responsibility ranged over much of the Science Museum Library. To David Bryden and to Tony Hall-Patch, as well as to the Science Museum's Director, Dr Neil Cossons, my thanks are due for permission to reproduce more of these splendid historic working drawings.

The selection and use of these drawings, and of the black and white photographs is necessarily an arbitrary decision in such a book as this. My main task, with the publisher, is to choose more from my dwindling supply of my own colour photographs taken between 1962-68. In the case of some wheel-arrangements, such as the Pacifics, one can display a reasonable percentage of the limited number of British 4-6-2s, as most were represented by members of the classes still in service at that time. Obviously the absolute converse applies to, shall we say, the 2-4-0. As this is by no whit intended to be a technical or learned tome, my selection of black-and-white pictures, and of the Science Museum drawings, with which to complement my own photographs, is arbitrary, unscientific and chronologically unco-ordinated. If this sounds like an apology, then so be it. As H. C. Casserley said in his foreword to his estimable *Locomotive Cavalcade 1920-1951*:

'It is a far cry from Johnson's lovely single-wheelers, typically representative of the grace of the later Victorian and Edwardian era, which were still to be found on the old Midland in the 1920s, and the new "Britannia" class of Pacific which have just seen the light of day in the year of grace 1951; and between these two extremes may be found a wealth of variety of endless fascination and interest to the "ferro-equinologist". For the benefit of readers unacquainted with this word — not I believe to be found in any dictionary — "ferro-equinologist" is, of course, the equivalent for "Study of the Iron Horse".'

To ferro-equinologists of my generation the name of H. C. Casserley, or indeed of Ransome-Wallis or Rixon Bucknall, is a name to be revered. They sought not to educate, let alone to bully or swamp: they sought to share their pleasure and enjoyment of railway enthusiasm. Even without a modicum of their knowledge, still I can at least aim to share their ambition.

This is just another book by a railway enthusiast for his peers.

The Simple Man's Guide to Wheels and their Movement

The size and number of wheels on a steam locomotive are principally related to the task that an individual class is designed to perform. Once the earliest classes gave way to more sophisticated types, higher speeds and heavier loads created problems in the translation of power and movement from machine to track. The words 'thrust', 'stability', 'stress', 'adhesion', 'torsion' and 'force' come to mind as factors determining the design criteria specified by the mechanical engineers.

Driving wheels exert pressure on the track: so bogies were introduced both to act as a guiding mechanism and to relieve the thrust of the leading flange of the first coupled wheel on the outer rail of a curve. On straight track, fast running induced 'nosing' which was alleviated by bogie wheels, or 'trucks'.

The more driving wheels an engine possesses, the greater is the distribution of weight on the rails. Coupling together pairs of driving wheels increases adhesion. Although small wheels permit minimum spacing, this can generate a high concentration of weight over a short length of track. In addition, wheelbase length and rigidity limit the minimum radius of track curvature which the locomotive can negotiate.

Simple problems of lack of space in the width of a locomotive on standard-gauge track (4ft 8½in) affect the size and number of cylinders from which power is transferred through the wheels to the track. More cylinders mean less 'hammer-blow' from locomotive to track, whilst the reciprocating parts of a two-cylinder engine exert maximum force on the locomotive's frame; this in turn can create an undesirable fore-and-aft movement. In mitigation, an overbalance is provided via rotating balance weights on the wheels: but this in turn creates a problem of 'lifting' the wheels from the rails when the crankpin is in the upper position. Thus, without an extended attempt at mechanical explanations well beyond my capability, it can be seen that the relation between wheels, cylinders and rails involve crucial design considerations.

Angles of cylinders relate to the need to limit stress. Ideally the centre-line of the pistons must be in line with the centre of the driving wheel. Whilst this presented few problems when small cylinders could be mounted outside the locomotives' frames but within the loading gauge, the advent of larger and more powerful locomotives required raised cylinders. The LMS 'Crab' 2-6-0 is an example of a clearly visible solution to this problem, whilst the GWR, with its more generous loading gauge, was less affected than the LMS, LNER and SR.

Finally, in this attempt at a potted version of 'The Simple Man's Guide to Wheels and their Movement', we should glance at the factors influencing which axle to drive, the main factor in which is the length of angularity of the connecting rod. This in turn is influenced by the position of the cylinders. To quote Arthur Tayler, to whom I am indebted for assistance in preparing these comments: 'Length is restricted by the ability to resist buckling as a strut in two planes at right angles; bending is due to inertia effects under centrifugal forces. The greatest thrust in the rod occurs at a low speed when pressure on the piston is at a maximum. The greatest bending load due to inertia is at high speed.' With three, four or five axles it is obviously preferable to drive as near as possible to the centre in order to control stress in the coupling rods, whilst keeping the length thereof within desirable limits.

Generally — there were of course exceptions — six- and ten-coupled engines were driven on the middle axle; eight-coupled the third coupled axle.

Right:
The Stanier rebuilds of the Fowler LMS 'Royal Scot' 4-6-0s were a significant development in the final flowering of British steam traction. Filthy engines, in cramped surroundings, on gloomy days, did not make for scintillating 'colour' photography, as is self-evident in the shot of No 46155 *The Lancer,* **at Willesden MPD on 5 July 1964. Her 5A shedplate would indicate a Crewe North engine, although allocated to Llandudno Junction (6G) officially at this date. The rebuilt 'Scots' shared virtually all the top link duties on the London Midland Region, until the coming of the diesels, with 'Princess Royal' and 'Coronation' Pacifics, one of which is behind** *The Lancer.* **Hand point levers, posts, poles, overhead lights and the looming of gloomy buildings were the hallmark of the steam engine shed, and the bane of railway photographers.**

11

Tyres are fixed to wheels under great pressure. At London Transport's Acton Works they press tyres at 20,000lb/sq in. Loose tyres are a rare occurrence indeed and this sequence of photographs illustrate a very unusual event — a tyre that had worked loose in service. The offending wheel was on the tender attached to BR Standard '5' 4-6-0 No 73030. *BR*

CHAPTER ONE

WHEELS THEMSELVES

'Although a simple component, the wheel and axle is of vital importance in the make-up of the locomotive and, from the point of view of safety, almost the most important, since any failure here can be attended by the most serious results.'

E. S. Cox

'My own experiences with wheels and axles and the conclusions I have arrived at coincide with those of the Author. . . .'

H. Holcroft
Lecture & Discussion,
Institution of Locomotive Engineers
31.10.35

Spinning wheels, panned photography, visible motion of man's mechanical mastery of movement — to the film producer they represent the obvious and visual manifestation of the steam locomotive at speed. Wheels are fundamental to most vehicular movement on land.

Wheels are fundamental to the steam locomotive, yet rarely if ever do they merit much attention as an item of interest in themselves. My library is stocked with railway books. Within these books are learned dissertations about almost every moving and working part. Valves and cylinders; brakes and pipes; tubes and doors — the list is endless. Yet who ever wrote about wheels? Naturally there are endless words about wheel-arrangements, wheel sizes, and everything one needs to know about the way to make wheels turn; but one searches in vain for more. Was there never a Walschaerts wheel: a Westinghouse wheel: a Salter wheel?

A wheel, I suppose, is inanimate, not a *mechanical* part in itself, so it merits no great attention. It is essentially external, but undoubtedly externally essential. Perhaps O. V. S. Bulleid would appreciate what I mean. He certainly gave visual vent to his thoughts about wheels. Surely the wheel deserves as much attention as, shall we say, the chimney? Think of the comments one has read about design and style of chimneys. Yes, I realise that the chimney is an integral part of the exhaust system, but its appearance is often the feature which excites most comment: 'The appearance of the locomotive was altered dramatically by the replacement of Gresley's gracious design by an ugly chimney that surely showed how Thompson wanted to disfigure his predecessor's elegant creation.' You have read that type of comment frequently.

Who *made* the wheels? How much attention to their appearance was given by the Chief Mechanical Engineer? What determined the number of spokes? Why did you need spokes at all?

As ever, the ignorant author turns for help to a member of the 'Brotherhood of Steam' for guidance on matters mechanical; and who better to whom to turn, than the founder-member of the Brotherhood — or at least the coiner of the phrase — namely Brian Haresnape. It was on a Sunday evening in December when I telephoned him at his home in Gassin near St Tropez. He was peeling garlic at the time. As ever, he was generous with his time, knowledgeable with his information and helpful with his advice.

Right:
Maunsell's 'W' class 2-6-4 tank engines were elusive, albeit small in number, only 15 being built. With 5ft 6in driving wheels and tractive effort of 29,450lb, they were powerful engines, designed more for steady acceleration with heavy loads, than for high speed running. They were mainly used, in their prime, for inter-railway cross-London freight traffic. On 11 May 1963, No 31917 was on shed at Feltham, one of five of the class to survive into 1964. For years a Norwood Junction (75C) engine, No 31917 went to Exmouth Junction for a few weeks in November 1962, and then returned to the London area, to end her days based at Feltham.

Brian and I discussed wheels. 'How many spokes in a steam-engine wheel?' he asked. He was uncertain and confirmed my view that the wheel has been neglected by railway authors. I mentioned his reference to 'Bulleid Firth-Brown type wheels' in his book *Bulleid Locomotives*, and he aimed me in the right direction for sources of information. Thus it was that my first enquiry was a letter to H. A. V. Bulleid. The mere thought of actually writing to the great man's son, lent a touch of excitement to my endeavours. Such is the magic of the great names of steam that it was not really a surprise or any kind of disappointment when H. A. V. Bulleid, son of O. V. S. Bulleid, replied that he could not update me with any new information since leaving the LMS in 1937. Nevertheless I shall keep his card as a valued memento.

If I was seriously to attempt to answer the soliloquous questions at the opening of the fourth paragraph of this chapter, then some modest research was required: or if research be too dignified a word, at least some investigation, or perhaps inquisitiveness was indicated. My first port of call was the Institution of Mechanical Engineers (IMechE), extremely conveniently situated near the Palace of Westminster. My thanks to Arthur Tayler, Manager, Railway Division, who immediately confirmed the arcane nature of my enquiry about wheels. After two lengthy sessions of searching and detective work, it seemed apposite to me to use for initial quotation the opening sentence of a Past President of the Institution of Locomotive Engineers, and scion of the closing of the steam era on British Rail, E. S. Cox, who in discussion of a paper on *Steel Wheels and Tyres*, presented to the Institution, stated that '. . . . the last handbook of the Institution listed only two papers, in all the life of the Institution, which had dealt mainly with wheels and tyres'. That was in 1960, the year of construction of the last steam locomotive for British Railways.

At this stage it is appropriate, if repetitive for me to reiterate my total ignorance of matters mechanical. To seek to bamboozle the readers of this book by attempting a scientific comparison between, and an analysis of, the merits of steel or cast-iron wheels in relation to the adhesion between wheel and rail and rate of retardation during an emergency stop, dependent on whether the brake-blocks were cast iron or composition, is outwith my scope. All I attempt is a cursory glance at 'the locomotive wheel'. Clearly the point where the wheel meets the rail, affects the riding properties. That steam locomotive wheels have tyres and that tyres themselves are doubtless of great interest to some people, is not in doubt; but for a superficial glance at a subject, clearly the wheels themselves, rather than their tyres, must be the subject under discussion. My protestations of ignorance of engineering matters caused me to seek an 'idiot's guide' to the meaning of 'wrought'. In the Oxford dictionary, the entry of 'wrought' refers one back to 'work': thus 'worked iron'='wrought iron'. Cast-iron is cast, when molten, into a mould. Steel is refined iron, with the carbon burned out by Bessemer's steel-making process. Driving wheels, as opposed to carrying wheels, transmit the driving force to the rails to produce motion.

However, the numerous documents that I have scoured have produced much more interesting material and, for me, new knowledge. From that same discussion paper referred to earlier, I learn from E. S. Cox that:

'Over two recent years, the total tyre breakages of British Railways had averaged nine per year of all the power units which they possessed, covering steam, diesel and electric locomotives and power bogies, the whole lot probably adding up to about a quarter of a million wheels in service. Of those eighteen cases of breakage in the two years, three only were due to defective material; fourteen of them were on old types of locomotive running out their time and having design features which were now superseded; and only three had been identified as taking place on modern locomotives containing new standard features of design such as had now been arrived at as best practice. That experience explained why British Railways, at any rate, had for some time taken up a very conservative view as regards innovations in wheel and tyre practice; it was against that background of security and relative satisfaction that this Paper was very timely in challenging complacency and in setting out all that the industry now had to offer.'

That 'very conservative view' regarding innovations in wheel (and tyre) practice are clearly based on the reasonable assumption of product-satisfaction. At the dawn of the railway era, however, experimentation with wheels was keen and rivalry fierce. In 1848, a certain H. S. Barlow compiled and arranged a *Comparative Account and Delineation of Railway Engine and Carriage Wheels*. Barlow was a Mancunian consulting engineer and patent agent, and he details the titles of the early wheel patents and quotes therefrom. The earliest patent for improvements in the construction of railway wheels was that granted to George Hawks of Gateshead; it is dated 6 November 1807. Other names that Barlow mentions include Thomas Rogers of Dublin — 28 November 1812; William Losh of Newcastle upon Tyne, and 'Geo. Stephenson, of Killingworth . . .', 30 September 1816; R. W. Brandling, Theodore Jones, W. Losh, John Hanson, Wm Frost, Henry Dircks, all registered their patents. Then, on 27 May 1840, was lodged another development. 'The nature of this invention consists in forming the outer or working surface of the tire (*sic*) of engine and carriage wheels of steel, which may be made of any

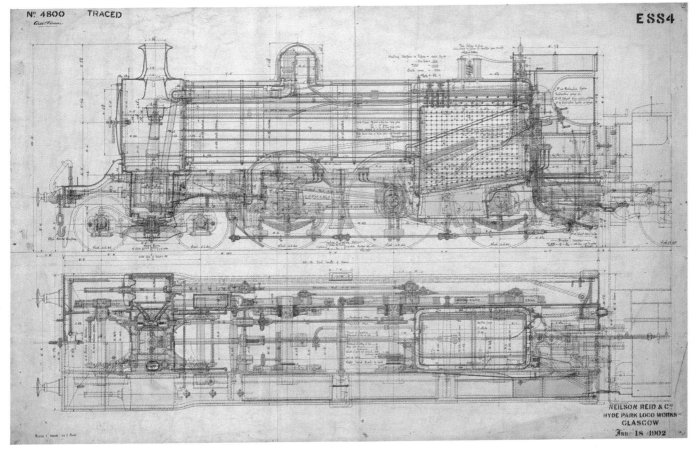

NEILSON REID & Cº
HYDE PARK LOCO WORKS
GLASGOW
June 18 1902

Above:

The working drawings obtained by the Science Museum from the North British Locomotive Company and its former constituents — Neilson, Neilson Reid, Dubs and Sharp Stewart — are of both historic significance and artistic joy to railway enthusiasts. My thanks again to Tony Hall-Patch for 'finding' them; to former Assistant Keeper David Bryden for 'preparing and photographing' them; and by no means least to Dr Neil Cossons, Director of the Science Museum, for enabling me to reproduce these treasures in this book. This modern-looking 4-6-0 was built by Neilson Reid for the Great Central Railway and the drawing is dated 18 June 1902.

Below:

The survival of three of W. G. Beattie's 2-4-0 well tanks has been told with sufficient regularity to make its repetition almost insulting to enthusiasts. For three members of a class introduced in 1874 to have survived into the 1960s is surprising; that two of the three, Nos 30585/7 were thereafter preserved, is not. That one, No 30586, lived for so long only then to be scrapped is sad. Thus this photograph, taken at Nine Elms on 25 May 1963, is of 'the one that got away' — not, sadly, to a life hereafter.

degree of hardness.' The patent was registered in the name of Mr D. Gooch.

The following year, 1849, saw Robert Stephenson in the chair of the Institution of Mechanical Engineers. In the report of the proceedings at the General Meeting, held in Birmingham on 25 April 1849, some discussion took place about wheels and tyres. Reference is made to recent railway accidents attributable to 'defects of railway wheels'. Of the four accidents to which reference is made, all relate to defective tyres. As Chairman of the meeting, Robert Stephenson remarked, in answering questions, that the life-span of the wheel was much greater than that of the tyre, which needed to be removed when only about a tenth of the life of the wheel was gone. In answering further comments from those at the meeting, he was moved to enthuse unequivocally about the advantages of wrought-iron as opposed to cast-iron wheels.

The evolution from cast-iron to wrought-iron wheels on Britain's early railways was hastened by the type invented by John Day in 1835. After the expiry of his patent in 1847, Day's wheel became almost universally used. Any attempt to research the evolution of the railway wheel leads to the subject of spokes and balancing. I do not propose to attempt anything other than to mention, in a few sentences for laymen, the relevance of both attributes. Spokes were the railway locomotive's evolutionary inheritance from the horse-drawn carriage wheel, and were an essential element in efficient braking, where air circulation is needed to cool braking achieved by friction. It may surprise readers as much as it surprised me to discover that London Transport, whose vehicles apply their brakes very frequently, still use spoked-wheel vehicles.

Balancing of steam locomotive driving wheels is needed to counteract the effect of off-centre masses, such as the crankpin. Dynamic balancing is needed to offset the effect of rotating masses such as the connecting rod. This 'dynamic augment', as it is known, relates to the hammer-blow effect on the track caused by the unbalanced force delivered to the track from the rotation of heavy parts of the wheel, at speed.

Hammer Blow is a neo-onomatopoeic phrase. Technically it is described as the variation in the load transmitted by the wheel to the rail which is produced by the vertical component of the centrifugal force arising from the portion, m lb, of the balance weight which is allocated to the reciprocating masses. The general expression for the load on the rail at any instant is expressed by a formula so beyond my comprehension that I can only refer those seeking technical knowledge, to page 292 of *Steam Locomotive Design: Data and Formulae* by E. A. Phillipson, published by the Locomotive Publishing Co Ltd in 1936.

If unqualified laymen find this incomprehensible, no such excuse should really have been accepted in the classic case of the Highland Railway's 4-6-0s designed by F. G. Smith. These fine engines, the 'River' class, had been built with a heavier deadweight than previous engines, but in the

Above:
The Highland Railway's 4-6-0s were elegant locomotives. After the Grouping, but still in HR livery, 'Clan' class No 49 *Clan Campbell* stands at Perth on 9 June 1924.

designer's knowledge that the law of 'dynamic augment' would ensure that, with proper wheel-balancing, the Highland track could well cope. It was not just the deadweight but the static loading per individual driving axle (or wheel) that alarmed the Chief Civil Engineer. He seemed to be unable to understand that the dynamic augment was actually reduced by the elimination of reciprocating balance and that the *total effect* on the track was thus less damaging than that caused by locomotives with a lower static axle load. Smith, however, was unable, perhaps due to personality problems, to persuade the Civil Engineer at Perth about the effect of dynamic augment. He was given a week in which to resign, or be dismissed. He resigned, the engines were sold to the Caledonian, which acquired six of the finest 4-6-0s ever built; and Smith's successor on the Highland then designed the 'Clan' class, with a lighter dead axle load, but a worse effect on the track — the effect of deadweight plus dynamic augment. Thus does history illustrate technology.

The previous paragraph has seen me straying beyond the bounds of my erudition into dangerous territory; let me return to the basic and the visual. In the latter category, wheel balance weights are indeed an obvious visual feature of the steam locomotive driving wheel; and different outward appurtenances can help to identify the works from which a locomotive emerged. With the Stanier '8F' 2-8-0s built at so many places (see Chapter 5), a really knowledgeable expert would identify a Doncaster-built '8F' from a Darlington-built example by the prominent rivet-heads on the driving wheel balance weights of the Doncaster-built engines, notwithstanding that both places turned out these LMS-designed machines with LNER standard disc wheels.

In due course in this tale of the wheel we shall come inevitably to Bulleid: were it not for him this chapter would probably not have been written. Like Churchward years before, he was an innovator who

sought knowledge from across the Atlantic. Lest it be thought that the elimination of the traditional spoked wheel was a manifestation of the final years of steam, it is my duty to point out that the Association of Manufacturers of Chilled Car Wheels was formed in Chicago in 1909. The majority of its members (and thus the bulk of the wheels they manufactured) were building freight wagons and passenger carriages, and locomotive tenders, rather than the locomotives themselves: indeed since its introduction in 1850 the chilled iron wheel has been the standard vehicle of transportation for rail-borne freight.

This digression into other types of rail wheels was not my intention, but as often happens, an inquisitive incursion into an unknown subject generates unsuspected interest. Amongst the reference books produced by Mr Arthur Tayler at the IMechE was *Steam Locomotion* by Edward Cecil Poultney: under the section heading 'WHEELS' is the following extract:

'Wheel centres used in modern locomotive practice are of different types or designs according as to whether they are for the coupled wheels, or are for the engine bogies or trucks, or for tenders.

'Coupled wheels may be of the spoked or disc pattern. The latter are of various different designs.

'Bogies or trucks have spoked wheel centres, or rolled steel centres, either with separate tyres or with the tyre or wheel tread portion rolled as part of the centre.

'For tenders, spoked centres, rolled steel centres with separate tyres, or rolled with the tyre or tread portion as part of the wheel are used.

'Generally, engine and tender wheels are of the spoked type fitted with separate tyres; the wheel centres are steel castings and, in some instances, they are iron castings.

'Rolled steel wheel centres for engine bogies or trucks and for tenders are steel forgings made by a special rolling process. It is not necessary to fit separate tyres because the wheel rim contour may be easily finished to a tyre section. However, centres of this type are often fitted with separate tyres, which has the advantage that they will last longer because the tyres can be renewed when required.

'When tyres are not used, the wheel tread can be reconditioned by being turned in a lathe, and, when turned down to scrapping size, the wheel must be renewed.'

The statement that 'wheel centres are steel castings and, in some instances, they are iron castings' indicates that steel castings were the norm: indeed that is the case. Thus, when Robin Riddles decided to use cast-iron wheel centres in his WD 'Austerity' 2-8-0, it seems that eyebrows were raised within the railway engineering world. In *The Locomotive* of 15 January 1943 appears the sentence: 'The reintroduction of this material after a gap of forty or fifty years (probably some of Webb's Coal Engines were the last English locomotives to be fitted with cast-iron coupled wheel centres) will not unnaturally

Above:

'Black Five' reliability; left-side cylinder, bogie wheels and slide-bar of No 45388, in the last week of British steam, at Rose Grove, Burnley, on 31 July 1968. If photographs could give off *smell* then this might merit entry in a competition to epitomise the appeal of the steam locomotive.

Above right:

'Colour photography' inside steam sheds in the closing years was almost a terminological inexactitude. Here, at Edge Hill Shed , Liverpool on 11 July 1965, Hughes-Fowler 'Crab' 2-6-0 No 42827 keeps company with two BR Standard '9F' 2-10-0s, Nos 92069 and 92092. Open smoke-box doors and the paraphernalia of the running shed, with engines undergoing light repairs, create their own atmosphere.

give rise to feelings of some trepidation and scepticism in the mind of engineers . . .' Riddles, of course, was building locomotives with an anticipated life-span of 5-10 years, rather than the 30-40 years of a 'peace-time' locomotive.

It should not be assumed, however, that all the earliest locomotives had cast-iron wheels. Indeed, a visit to the Science Museum in South Kensington — highly recommended when you have been to the National Railway Museum in York — will enable you personally to verify that *Puffing Billy*, vintage 1813, has wrought-iron driving wheels. *Rocket* wheels had wooden centres with wrought-iron tyres, whilst the wheels on *Sanspareil* are of cast-iron. Lest one deludes oneself into believing that cast-iron went

out with the Ark, John Coiley reminded me that in the 1950s the Ford Motor Co were using cast-iron crankshafts.

Whilst the initial cost of a solid, as opposed to spoked, wheel is lower, the spoked wheel was very much the most widely used on British locomotives, as is self-evident. Rapid improvement in steel-making techniques coincided with the demise of steam, which ensured that an ever-increasing proportion of today's railway wheels are made by the basic electric arc process. However, this is not only too technical, but is irrelevant to the British steam era with which I am concerned. If you are seriously interested in all this, then try reading the aforementioned paper entitled *Steel Wheels and Tyres*, presented to the Institution of Mechanical Engineers on 26 April 1960.

Cast-iron wheels were initially made in many foundries, often indeed in small premises. A fascinating insight into the way in which early wheelwrights tackled the challenge of the steam engine, may be gained from this hand-written letter.

Mr Mawson   *Liverpool*
Sir,

I have often thought of writing a few lines to you, to give you some information how I am getting on here — am happy to say that I am very well in health and have been so ever since I came to Liverpool. I have made a pair of Locomotive Engine Wheels for the Great Western Railway, an undertaking I assure you of great responsibility being the first of the kind ever made in the Works in which they were made. The inclosed

is a rough sketch of the wheel, but you must not judge of the job by the drawing, as my hand has been more accustomed to heavy work than to drawings. You will be surprised when I tell you that the wheel is one solid piece of wrought iron the spokes and flange being all one solid piece without a single joint, it will not be necessary for me to explain the method I took to manage the job. Suffice it to say that each wheel was welded together in 140 parts, and if one single welding had been imperfect the wheel would have been spoiled altogether, however I was so successful that should you have seen the wheel after it was finished I could defy you to find out one single part where it had been welded, neither could any Blacksmith know in what way it had been made unless they had seen it before it was put together, each wheel had 28 spokes they are 6½in apart at the flange or rim and touching each other in the center they had to be leveled so as to come down each end of the naphe otherwise there would not have been room for them, so that you may consider it as double spoked they also run up to the sides of the rim alternately so that it had a very strong appearance. The naphe was 2ft diameter and 11in thick so that to look at it you might almost pronouce it everlasting, one wheel weighed about 1 ton without the tier or hoop. I do not wish you to understand that I was the first to make these kind of wheels, they are made in Manchester and two or three more places in the country, however I can say that I have been the sole contriver of an apparatus for taken this massy wheel in and out of the fire. While putting it together and the plan answered so remarkably until that 2 men always took it out of the fire and placed it on the anvil where I wanted it with as much ease and readiness as they could have lifted a piece of iron 6lb weight. I had 5 men assisting me when putting it together but only 2 when preparing the parts, the naphe is cast in the middle, I may just observe that we had not a crane strong enough to lift it into the fire which caused me to fix upon the other plan and it answered much better than any crane could do, my wages were advanced after I began with the job. I had also 38 more wheels to make upon the same principles but much smaller in size, am sorry to say that just before I had the second wheel finished the Works stopped and have never commenced yet, Mr Marshall one of the partners joined another concern at Derby and would have paid the expences of removing myself and family if I would go to Derby and finish the order of wheels but however I could not make up my mind to go. I have been working the last 8 weeks a little out of Liverpool but am expecting a situation very shortly in the town, I have been out of work from this shut up for 5 weeks and was laid up through a misfortune with my finger for other 4 weeks so that you may judge that has rather made against me, there are many other kinds of wrought iron wheels made here for wagons but those large ones are a first rate job the tiers made at Wigan and steeled at the outside.

I received a letter from my sister last week and am glad to hear that my mother is as well as can be expected. I can only thank you again at the present for the kind attention you have always paid to her welfare and would still pray you to give a look after her when ever convenient, please give my respects to your brothers Thomas and Isaac and Miss Mawson.

I remain yours respectfully,

Thomas Tunnian

Brian Haresnape, as usual a source of detailed information, tells us of the WD 'Austerity' 2-8-0s in his *Ivatt and Riddles Locomotives* that 'high-duty cast iron was used for the coupled wheel centres except for the third, main pair, which were steel castings; all the centres were made from similar patterns'. He goes on to say that 'The leading truck and the tender wheels were of chilled cast iron, but

following early troubles with this feature, rolled forged wheels were substituted'. He attributes these decisions to economies in production, rather than to the assumption of a short life. Incidentally, recalling the controversy surrounding those Highland Railway 4-6-0s, it is worth noting that the 'Austerity' 2-8-0's wheels had balance weights that were cast integrally with the centres and no allowance was made for the reciprocating parts.

It was assumed in *The Locomotive* article referred to above that Riddles' decision was taken because a short life-span was anticipated for his 'Austerities', notwithstanding that much hard work for these locomotives was inevitable, often on inferior permanent way. At about this time, the first

---

Right:
Whilst tests by Gresley on his own Great Northern Pacifics, following the 1923 Grouping, ensured that they rather than the Raven North-Eastern 4-6-2s would form the backbone of the fledgling LNER's express passenger fleet, only a Gresley sycophant would deny the imperious magnificence of Raven's engines. This official Darlington photograph of North Eastern Railway No 2400 (later named *City of Newcastle*) makes comment superfluous.

Below right:
A period piece that I could not resist. London and North Western Railway 'Claughton' class 4-6-0 No 2416 detains two contemporary young ladies from crossing the line, as it speeds a down LNWR express at Morecambe South Junction. The stock is as interesting and as typical as the locomotive of its era.

Above:
Compare this photograph with the manufacturer's drawings, reproduced on pages 76/7. Highland Railway 'Jones Goods' No 116 looks as though it has received the attention of

jolly young things with paint brushes known in the Sloane Rangers Handbook as 'Marblers'. The fancy paintwork detracts from rather than enhances the elegant lines of Britain's first 4-6-0.

14 May 1964 sees LMS Fairburn 2-6-4T No 42099 on the move at Watford Shed. That the BR lined-out livery and emblems are colourfully visible rates this as a comparatively clean engine by contemporary standards. Notice the catenary behind the locomotive's bunker; harbinger of the end of steam at a shed that closed in March 1965. The Fowler, Stanier and Fairburn 2-6-4Ts all had 5ft 9in driving wheels, 1in larger than the BR Standard '4MT' machines which were nevertheless firmly based on the LMS engines.

Above:

The poor condition of this photograph, obtained from the owner of the collection of early Baldwin negatives, was outweighed by its interest, for inclusion. Catalogued only as 'Lickey Inclined Plane, England', the information below the picture states 'BIRMINGHAM AND GLOUCESTER RAILWAY CAPT W. S. MOORSON, Eng^r. The Philadelphia Engine, ascending the Plane, rising one in 37 with a train of loaded wagons: the total weight moved 74 tons — the maximum speed 9¾ miles per hour.' The locomotive is a 4-2-0 with four-wheeled tender. The B&GR had 40 American-designed 4-2-0s built between 1838 and 1840. In *The British Railway Locomotive 1803-1853*, published by the Science Museum, there appears as Plate 19, a 4-2-0 illustrated from an original water-colour, described as 'probably Birmingham and Gloucester Railway 1839-42', and noted as 'probably built by the Nasmyth firm in England'. There are similarities but material differences between the locomotive illustrated here and that in the Science Museum booklet, enough to justify the supposition that this is one of the original American-built engines. Obscurity surrounds the history of these locomotives.

American 2-8-0s — known as the 'S160s' — were arriving in Britain, but these locomotives were fitted with cast-steel driving wheels. Not a great deal has been written in British railway books about these engines. They are, naturally, well documented in R. Tournet's book *United States Army Transportation Corps Locomotives*, but the section on the 'S160s' makes virtually no reference to the wheels.

From locomotives whose wheels attracted little or no attention, we turn now to perhaps the most interesting development in British steam locomotive wheels — the work of O. V. S. Bulleid on the Southern Railway. Happily, many of his Pacifics have been preserved. Ever an innovator, Bulleid took nothing for granted, spokes on locomotive wheels being merely one traditional engineering feature he challenged. Thus, the disc, or box mode of wheel emerged in 1941 from Eastleigh on the 'Merchant Navy' class. The first formal reference I have found to such a wheel, in this country, was in a question by one K. C. C. Hunter to E. S. Cox during the discussion of the paper presented by the latter to the Institution of Locomotive Engineers, to which I have already referred. At the Institution's Birmingham meeting on 13 November 1935, Mr Hunter asked 'Can the Author say whether there was any future for the American box spoke cast steel wheel?' E. S. Cox described the box spoke as a 'new departure' and added that 'very little is known about it over here. It seems to have the virtue of giving an even support to the tyre all round, but might prove rather heavy when applied to British practice'. These words make interesting reading when juxtaposed alongside an article in the 15 January 1943 edition of *The Locomotive*, where the author notes that 'the disc wheel does at least provide a regular and continuous support for the rim, and this is of particular importance if the rims are tyred, as they would be for coupled wheels'. Further comment illustrated the divergence of opinion amongst engineers about box-pattern wheels. O. V. S. Bulleid never shrank either from innovation or controversy.

The 1938 edition of *Locomotive Cyclopedia of American Practice* indicates that the realities of railway operation rather than the fascination of pure science motivated the development of, amongst other things, the Boxpok wheel: inevitably the bastardisation of the English language, so much a feature of American 'civilisation', converted 'box spoke' into 'Boxpok'. Higher speeds, heavier train loads, greater density of traffic — all were features as the world emerged from the depression of the early 1930s; combined with the inevitable problems of track and road-bed maintenance, the Boxpok driving and indeed trailing wheels were seen as a factor of the greatest importance. In a feature in the publication to which reference is made above, there appears, in an article by General Steel Castings Corporation, the following:

'Experience in making the old spoke-type driving wheel has demonstrated that this design does not lend itself to the best foundry conditions, and with the Boxpok design it is possible to produce better castings. On account of the better and more economical distribution of metal, the Boxpok driving wheel centers are stronger, both laterally and also in the rim section.

'The box section rim construction, with supporting walls on both sides, has much greater strength and a more uniform tire support and is designed to prevent out-of-round wheels and flat spots, increasing tire mileage and reducing wheel maintenance.

'The Boxpok design also has greater strength to resist high piston thrusts, lateral forces and rail impacts, as well as an improved construction between crank pin hub and rim. The large openings give adequate accessibility for inspection and lubrication.

'The Boxpok driving wheel has been widely adopted for both new and existing power. Most of the locomotives recently built, have been equipped with Boxpok wheel centers on all drivers. Many roads have also applied Boxpok main wheels to existing power to replace spoke wheels, due to failures or out-of-round rims, and in some instances,

---

Below:
Hiding, not posing, might seem more appropriate for the railwaymen involved with this embarrassment. The hurt expression carried by this derailed North British 4-4-0 reminds us of the express passenger duties from the 'racing days' of what for many years was the wheel-arrangement of the premier type of Scottish locomotive.

27

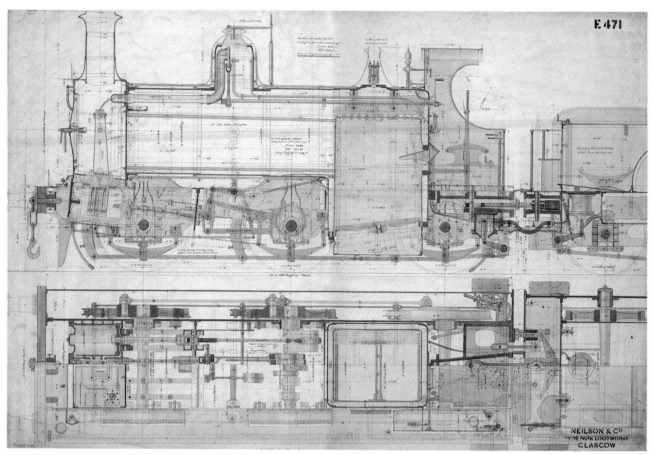

E 471

NEILSON & Co
HYDE PARK LOCO WORKS
GLASCOW

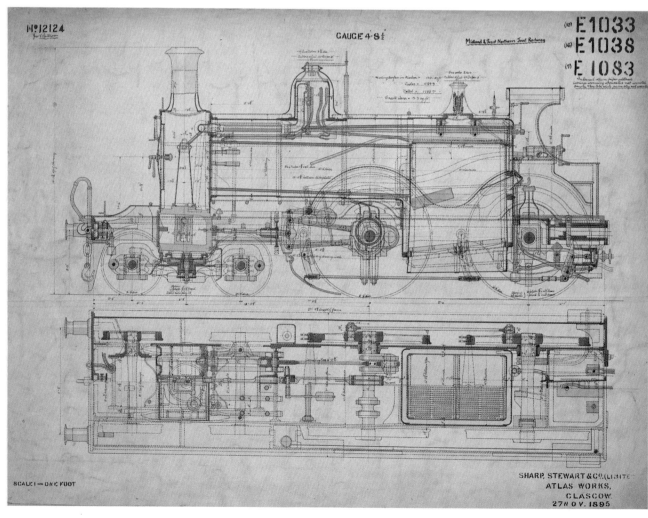

No 12124

GAUGE 4·8½

Midland & Great Northern Joint Railway

(10) E 1033
(16) E 1038
(7) E 1083

SCALE 1 = ONE FOOT

SHARP, STEWART & Co (LIMITED)
ATLAS WORKS,
GLASCOW
27 NOV. 1895

Top left:
Within the timespan from which these plans come, it has not been possible to include an example of every wheel-arrangement to correlate with the chapters of this book; and I have arbitrarily decided which plans to feature. Inevitably from that era there is a preponderance of four and six-coupled locomotives, with the 0-6-0 predominating amongst the engines built for British customers. This undated but colourful drawing is as decorative as it is informative. The only records available at the Science Museum relating to these drawings are handwritten lists of skimpy information, which denote this, No E471, as built in 1878 for the S&DJR.

Bottom left:
The splendid stylish lines of this 4-4-0, built by Sharp Stewart for the Midland & Great Northern Joint Railway, encapsulate the panache of one of Britain's minor but proudly independent railways. That Sharp Stewart built for customers around the world, with a variety of gauges, is illustrated by the heading 'GAUGE 4ft 8½in' above the dome. Wheels, on this design, were by no means merely something on which the locomotive ran.

Above:
Wheels in the afternoon sun, in those far-off days when the sun shone in springtime. On 20 March 1966, as Prospective Conservative Parliamentary Candidate for Birkenhead, I had heeded the sensible advice to 'get away from it all' on the Sundays during the election campaign. On a foray in search of steam, first stop was Mold Junction MPD, where the bright light illuminating Standard '5' 4-6-0 No 73140 highlighted the Caprotti valve-gear as well as the 6ft 2in wheels. This is the first of my Mold Junction photographs to be published. Other steam on shed that day included LMS 'Black Five' 4-6-0, LMS '3F' 0-6-0T, and '9F' 2-10-0 (one of which is visible ahead of No 73140), whilst a Stanier tender also basks in the sun.

Below:
Only five 'H16' 4-6-2T locomotives were built. Designed by Urie and designated '6F' by BR, they were introduced by the LSWR in 1921 for heavy freight traffic. All spent their lives at Feltham, until withdrawal, which fate befell all five, including No 30516, in November 1962. Here, some six months later, on 11 May 1963, she stoically awaits her fate; that numberplate would be a valuable trophy, but as yet this is still not realised by BR. Behind the 'H16', the smokebox of 'W' 2-6-4T No 31923 is visible. I wish I had an LSWR wheel . . .

on tow-wheel engines, to improve counterbalance conditions.'

These quotations from an article relate to US practice. A prime reason for the adoption of Boxpok wheels in the USA was the need for added strength due to the higher driving axle loads than those pertaining in Europe; up to 40% higher, indeed. The wheels illustrated in the accompanying article, and indeed those illustrating articles on subsequent pages of the same publication, featuring wheels from the Baldwin Locomotive Works of Philadelphia and the Sullin Steel Co of St Louis, bear a clear resemblance to Bulleid's 'Merchant Navy' wheels, and indeed to the current production wheels in use on the Chinese 'QJ' class 2-10-2 still being built at Datong in Shanxi Province in the People's Republic. (At the time of writing, production of the 'QJ' 2-10-2 is sporadic, but the 'JS' 2-8-2, with the same wheels, is still in progress.)

That Robin Riddles chose not to use any Boxpok-type wheels on any of his BR Standard steam locomotives may have been due to many factors; he may not even have considered them. How I wish I had asked him about this during the course of my meeting and 'interview' with him at his home in Calne, Wiltshire, in 1981. Riddles was not Bulleid's most fervent admirer. Nevertheless, Bulleid could — and doubtless did — claim that there were good reasons other than American experience on which to base his innovative decision. His Boxpok-type wheels eliminated the need for retaining rings, set bolts and other metal, as well as fulfilling the advantages foreseen by E. S. Cox; the result was a wheel some 12% lighter than similarly-sized spoked wheels.

My use of the phrase 'Boxpok-type' is not coincidental. Whilst the parentage of the research and development was undeniable, the reality of production was that Bulleid, in conjunction with the steel manufacturers Thomas Firth and John Brown,

developed what are known as the 'Bulleid Firth Brown', or 'BFB', wheels. D. L. Bradley in his excellent *Locomotives of the Southern Railway* goes so far as to imply that the wheels that evolved were different from their Boxpok cousins because the designers 'made sufficient variations to avoid payment of royalties'.

In mitigation of any suggestion as to Bulleid's motives or methods — and to me as a layman he has always seemed an exciting and adventurous innovator — it may be worth quoting his own words, in defence of his wheels. These appear as part of 'Some Notes on the "Merchant Navy" Class Locomotives of the Southern Railway' and appeared in the Proceedings of the IMechE in 1945:

'The most obvious departure from traditional practice is to be seen in the wheel centres used throughout these engines and tenders. The usual locomotive wheel consists of a cast steel spoked centre on which is shrunk a rolled steel tyre, and it has undergone little alteration since the earliest days.

'When the rims of spoked wheels in the shops for retyring are examined, flexing between the spokes is revealed by the condition of the rim and the inside of the tyre, resulting in fretting corrosion of the tyre. The stresses set up in a rim when a tyre is shrunk on were investigated by polarised light on celluloid models in the laboratory at Ashford and showed great variation from spoke to spoke.

'A locomotive wheel has not only to support the vertical load but has to have considerable lateral strength to support the heavy thrust of the flange against the rail when taking curves. Lightness too is important to keep down the kinetic energy and unsprung weight.

'Eventually, with the collaboration of Messrs Thomas Firth and John Brown, the wheel known as the "BFB" type was evolved. Under polarised light the models showed that the stresses in the rim inside the tyre had been equalised.'

Left:
Fine photographer, fine wheel, fine locomotive: Maurice Earley's affinity to Reading and the Great Western are encapsulated by his 1958 picture of the centre driving-wheel of 'Castle' class 4-6-0 No 5084 *Reading Abbey*, **at this date and until withdrawal in July 1962 an Old Oak Common engine.**

My nervousness about my ability to write this chapter, confronted my temerity in deciding so to do. However, two eminent experts have been immensely kind in editing my efforts, and in helping me to eradicate some of the more glaring errors. To Dr John Coiley, Curator of the National Railway Museum, and to Arthur Tayler of the Institution of Mechanical Engineers I am immensely grateful. Mr Tayler indeed gave the chapter a 'committee stage' line-by-line examination, and added some comments of his own. He will not, I trust, mind my quoting him *verbatim* about Bulleid and his BFB wheels:

'The chief reason for adopting the BFB wheels was the better tyre support they gave. It enabled the SR to dispense with the "Gibson" ring usually employed to retain the tyre in place and use a "double-lip" fastening. However, this latter was later used on the BR Standards, so it was not a fundamental feature of the BFB wheel.'

Then, referring to the third paragraph of the four that I have quoted above, Mr Tayler says that it:

'. . . shows the lack of understanding of wheel and rail relationship. If the tyre profile is correct and if the wheel head is not unduly worn there should never be contact between rail and flange except in extremely sharp curve negotiation. The bad lateral behaviour of many steam locomotives *did* result at times in flange-rail contact, often heavily.'

Some minor experimentation appears to have been undertaken by Bulleid with his BFB wheels on the 'Merchant Navy' class. The coupled wheels of 2IC18 (later BR No 35018) *British India Line* were originally fabricated from separate pieces welded together, rather than being cast whole as with the other 29 members of the class. However, in April 1947 those wheels were removed and replaced with the standard variety.

Bulleid, as with anyone who challenges accepted wisdom, drew and still draws criticism from his contemporaries and successors. He has been accused of most 'crimes', from extravagance in wartime to extreme thrift, in creating the 'Q1' 0-6-0 regardless of appearance. Regarding his BFB wheels, it is perhaps worth mentioning that the Southern Railway possessed no steel foundry and he would have been forced to 'buy in' from sub-contractors. Welded wheels, however, could be made 'in-house'.

In the light of the mechanical difficulties encountered with Bulleid's Pacifics, and the controversy that surrounded them, it seems that the BFB wheels were one of the few features which were free from aggravation. During rebuilding of the 'Merchant Navy', 'West Country' and 'Battle of Britain' locomotives almost everything must have come under scrutiny, but the trouble-free wheels survived intact. Bulleid's 'Q1' 0-6-0 joined his Pacifics as the only British steam locomotives to be constructed with box-spoke wheels. That all British steam locomotives built after Bulleid's machines reverted to the spoked wheel is not to condemn either Bulleid as the author of an unsuccessful experiment with wheels, or to castigate Thompson, Peppercorn, Fairburn, Ivatt, Hawksworth or Riddles — his contemporaries and successors — as old-fashioned. It is perhaps, bearing in mind Riddles' use of cast-iron on his 'Austerities' for the first time since Webb on his coal engines, merely to illustrate the enduring nature of 'the wheel' rather than its flamboyance as an item of engineering, that accounts for there being so little written about wheels, as such. Yet the fact remains that wheel-arrangement is the descriptive adjective by which individual types of locomotive are identified. It is not the number of cylinders, or tubes, but the number of wheels that counts.

Above:
On 22 August 1967 Stoke shed was already closed, and a scene of death and dereliction. Locomotives awaited their final journey, which clearly in the case of the Stanier 'Black Five' No 45050 was not going to be under her own steam. A momentary shaft of sunshine highlights not only the wheels, but the connecting rods on the running plate fastened together with rope. Smokebox number and shedplates have been removed; no doubt somebody somewhere keeps these mementoes of a member of an outstanding class of locomotive. 45050 was officially withdrawn in August 1967 and scrapped at Cohens of Kettering. Stoke Shed even in decay was a remarkable sight. The largest and most important on the North Staffordshire Railway, it trumpeted the vitality and self-confidence of the day. Built in 1852, it was architecturally outstanding but, over the years, demeaned by the shacks and lean-tos which it acquired. The shed finally closed two weeks before this photograph was taken.

Below:
Clean, green BR Standard '5' 4-6-0 No 73095 stands dead outside Croes Newydd Shed on Sunday 20 March 1966, although coal tops her BR1C tender. Surface rust on the centre driving wheel is aligned with the wheel's balance weight, whilst her chimney is capped, indicating an engine in store; notice the wires holding the chimney plug in place.

CHAPTER TWO

0-6-0

Let us start here, for no other reason than so to do releases me from the bondage of chapter order regulated by declension. My perversity encourages me to discard the obvious choice of writing first about the most powerful machines, and then descending, by wheel-arrangement, tractive effort or other arbitrary form of measurement, to the smallest, most humble — the adjectives are predictable — locomotives qualifying for a mention.

As a generalisation, the type of locomotive, and indeed its wheel-arrangement, was likely, but not certain, to determine the environment in which it worked, and in which it could be seen and photographed. It was unusual to see a Pacific at work in a marshalling yard; equally one did not expect to see a 2-8-2T at the head of a rake of Pullman coaches in full flight. Perhaps, therefore, the 0-6-0 tender engine is an appropriate choice for the first chapter, as virtually all the Pre-Grouping companies and certainly the 'Big Four' made extensive use of such machines. It could reasonably be described as the workhorse of the British steam railway era.

The obvious juxtaposition of wheels on vehicles, is one at each corner. In locomotive terms, therefore, the 0-4-0 wheel-arrangement was inevitably how it all started. The phrase 'wheel-arrangement' had yet to be invented. In the earliest days, both engine and 'tender' — another word that came later — were of the most basic. After the first experimental locomotives, the 2-2-2 wheel-arrangement, with massive driver, became the early vogue, as speed was equated to diameter. It was only a matter of time before the first coupled driving wheels appeared; the GWR had 12 on its books by 1841. It was in the following year, 1842, that the Great Western provided itself with its first 0-6-0 locomotives. All were Broad Gauge engines.

That the 0-6-0 was the first six-coupled wheel-arrangement — so far as I am aware — is hardly surprising. What is noteworthy, however, is that it

retained its vogue to become the standard British freight type; and its longevity far outlasted its other early contemporaries. A brief glance at the GWR 0-6-0 stock, compared to those other early engines, well illustrates the point.

	1842*	1862		1893	1923	1948	1964
2-2-2	111	71* 56	} 127	101	—	—	—
2-4-2	18	8* 45	} 53	197	65	3	—
0-6-0	4	128* 138*	} 266	585	373	183	15

*=Broad Gauge.

The very phrase 'Dean Goods' is almost part of Britain's railway folklore, describing a class of engines that for reliability, versatility and longevity had few peers. Indeed these qualities brought their own problems, through the GWR's reluctance to scrap locomotives still providing an adequate service although long in the tooth. The result inevitably was an ageing fleet of 0-6-0s both from Dean and indeed Armstrong. With Churchward's era at Swindon came a fleet of new 2-6-0s and 2-8-0s for freight and intermediate main line work, and the inevitable and consequential demise of many, but by no means all, of the old 0-6-0s. Thus in the early years of the century the GWR possessed a declining fleet of locomotives of this wheel-arrrangement, resulting from Churchward's supreme work as Chief Mechanical Engineer, which saw him equipping the Great Western with modern motive power into the Grouping of 1923. The LMS at this date found itself in a very different position as far as the 0-6-0 was concerned; the LNER had a large fleet of Gresley engines; whilst on the Southern, the final manifestation of British 0-6-0 was yet to come.

Above:
Photographs of one moving train, taken from another, are often poor, and this is no exception. En route from Manchester to St Pancras on 1 April 1964, I caught Rowsley (16J) LMS '4F' 0-6-0 No 44172 on a typical duty, south of Peak Forest. The locomotive was, in fact, withdrawn the following month: one of my very few black-and-white photographs. *Author*

As the basis of this book is my colour photographs, it is inevitable that each chapter will tend to concentrate, in respect of each wheel-arrangement, on those locomotives still in service in the final years of steam. This in turn means that my comments tend to relate to that period. It is no part of my intent to seek to write a historical analysis, let alone an engineering appreciation of all, some, or any particular engines.

Having, then, looked at the 0-6-0 on the GWR, and seen its partial eclipse through the Churchward era, it is a tribute to the value, versatility and longevity of the 0-6-0 to note the Great Western's need for a new machine as the last of the Dean and Armstrong locomotives were displaced from main line duties. Thus in 1930 there emerged from Swindon Collett's '2251' class 0-6-0. Although clearly 'Great Western' it was distinctly different in appearance from other GW locomotives. Construction continued up to, during and after World War 2, the final engine emerging from Swindon Works in 1948, a mere 10 years before the class suffered its first withdrawal. They were quite nippy, could exceed 60mph without blinking, and were very much mixed-traffic engines.

If the GWR was not heavily dependent on the 0-6-0, the LMS certainly was. Whilst Collett was introducing the '2251' class, many of the elderly Kirtley double-framed 0-6-0s were still hard at work on the LMS, particularly on the Midland lines north of Wellingborough. Indeed, the constituent companies, large and small, contributed every size and shape of this wheel-arrangement. However unglamorous, unimaginative or unspectacular, it is not unreasonable to claim for the LMS the title of '0-6-0 champion'. The Class 4, later '4F', introduced by Henry Fowler on the Midland Railway in 1911, is perhaps the most familiar face of the 20th century 0-6-0. Built in batches until 1922 it became an immediate choice, at the Grouping, for standardisation on the emergent LMS.

As a 'spotter' and railway enthusiast with camera, it was always with anticipation that one hoped for a Midland rather than a LMS '4F' to appear, although my inexpert eye found identification far easier through checking the number in my Ian Allan number book than by visual recognition. '4Fs' poured out of Crewe, Derby, Horwich and St Rollox, as well as from the works of three private builders, between 1924-28. Indeed, it is not widely realised that even in the Stanier years these warhorses emerged from Crewe and Derby (whence the last appeared in 1941) some 30 years after the prototype, with its fluted side rods, tall boiler mountings and Ramsbottom safety valves, first saw the light of day.

If the GWR spurned the 0-6-0 whilst the LMS spawned them, then certainly it is not this pedestrian wheel-arrangement that springs to mind at the mention of Nigel Gresley. Yet his 'J38' and 'J39' Goods Engines — the latter really an enlarged version of the former — which appeared in 1926, again illustrated the need of the Post-Grouping railways of Britain for 0-6-0 locomotives. They may not have been Gresley's *pièces de résistance* as far as his admirers were concerned; they were, however, amongst the best of the type ever produced. The 'J39' became Gresley's most numerous class, 289 engines being built between 1926 and 1941, the final members of the class emerging from Darlington

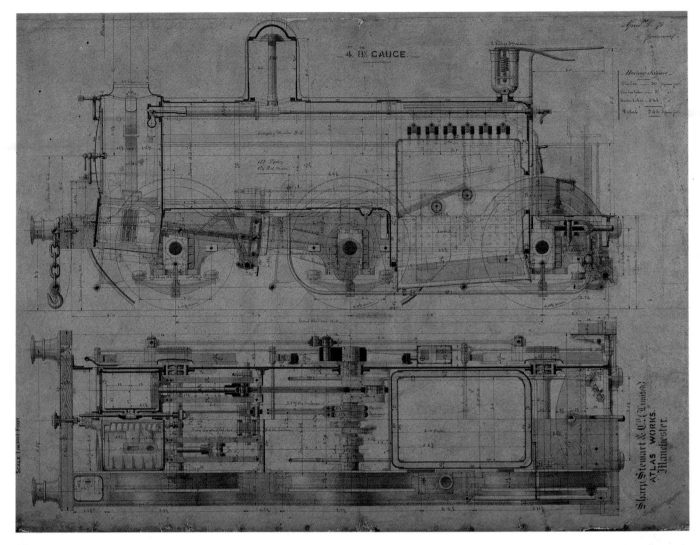

Above:
Having previously explained the preponderance of drawings of the classic early wheel-arrangements, my choice for this chapter fell on the Sharp Stewart 0-6-0. The drawing is dated 5 April 1875. Note in the bottom right-hand corner 'Sharp Stewart & Co (Limited) Atlas Works, Manchester'. Note also the splendid coupling at the front of the engine.

works almost contemporaneously with the emergence of the last '4Fs' on the LMS.

Indeed, the 'J38' and 'J39' may not have been the 'glamour girls' of Gresley's stud; but they outlasted many of his passenger locomotives. The 'J38s', originally designed for use in Scotland, were so well regarded there that LNER and later BR Scottish Region management insisted on keeping them. Three of the class lasted right up to the end of steam in Scotland in 1967. No 65930 went through Inverurie Works in 1963, at a time when most former LNER engines were being hauled off to the scrapyards. Indeed, albeit only 35 strong, the 'J38s' actually outlasted their 'developed offspring' the 'J39s', the entire class of which were withdrawn in the three years 1959-62.

The final manifestation of what was perhaps the most popular, versatile and numerous British

wheel-arrangement, flowered on the Southern Railway and was conceived by Richard Maunsell. In fact the first 'Q' class locomotive did not emerge until after his retirement. Of these engines, Brian Haresnape, in his excellent book *Maunsell Locomotives*, says '. . . Maunsell's successor, O. V. S. Bulleid, is on record as stating that, had he arrived upon the scene earlier, he would have stopped construction of such an uninspired and pedestrian design'.

Be that as it may, the Southern too had a need to replace a string of ancient Pre-Grouping 0-6-0s. As with the Collett and Gresley engines, there emerged a new design to cope with a traditional locomotive requirement. As with the GWR and LNER locomotives, the 'Qs' were used on occasional passenger work, but less frequently than the 'J39s' and certainly less so than the '2251s'. From time to time Bulleid and SR experimented with the 'Qs': the most notable innovation was the multiple-jet blastpipe, and the most visible was the chimney associated therewith. One of the class, No 30549, ran with a variety of chimneys from original, to Bulleid large-diameter, to stovepipe, to BR Standard, and in April 1963 when I photographed her at Redhill Shed, back to stovepipe, albeit a slightly less ugly

Above:
Reading (GW) MPD's '2251' class 0-6-0 No 2261 at home on 4 May 1963. The last GWR class of this wheel-arrangement — even this 1930 Collett design illustrates the difficulty of creating a graceful 0-6-0. The '2251' class always seemed the odd man out in the family of Great Western motive power. With 5ft 2in wheels — 1in smaller than those of the MR/LMS '4F' — they were classified '3MT' by British Railways and, like many locomotives of this wheel-arrangement, they made up in reliability and trouble-free performance what they lacked in glamour and style. Another member of the class faces No 2261, but I failed to record the number. No 2261 was withdrawn in September 1964.

Below:
LMS '4F' 0-6-0 No 44460, already withdrawn, stands in the open at Newton Heath on 3 December 1964, with class sister No 44431 alongside. Note the piece of wood wedged between the rail and the centre driving wheel. The yellow stripe was painted on all engines forbidden, on safety grounds, from working south of Crewe following electrification southwards therefrom on the West Coast main line. The MR/LMS '4F' was the absolute epitome of the British 0-6-0 freight engine.

version than that with which she had been adorned some years earlier.

The last class of 0-6-0 to appear on Britain's railway system probably earned more adjectives than any of its predecessors. Described by O. S. Nock as 'indescribably ugly', Bulleid's 'Q1' was undoubtedly the most distinctive design of an essentially pedestrian type of steam engine not inherently formed for elegance. If one thinks for a moment, bogies and trailing trucks enable a designer to create a more aesthetically pleasing shape than can ever be possible with a locomotive all of whose wheels are the same size. On the basis, therefore, that locomotive beauty necessitates flamboyance and/or weight and that wartime was austerity time; plus the fact that the Southern's Civil Engineer wanted a locomotive not exceeding 54 tons all-up weight, an ugly locomotive seemed inevitable. Bulleid did not

disappoint, although there lingers the suspicion that he took an impish pleasure in creating a machine truly memorable by its ugliness.

In fact, Bulleid combined the discipline of wartime frugality with the basic principles of locomotive engineering, to produce an engine with a tractive effort of 30,000lb and very wide route availability. The objective was to cover the need for hauling unexpectedly heavy wartime freight traffic on secondary lines to the southern coast, thus avoiding London, which in peacetime saw little, and then only light, freight traffic, most of which was handled by ancient 0-6-0s until the outbreak of hostilities.

Whatever the traditionalists may have had to say about the 'Q1's' appearance, there were few critics of their performance. Indeed, the main attributes of its ugliness, such as the absence of running-plate or splashers, were features warmly welcomed by the Southern's running department, for whom ease of access to inside cylinders and other parts meant less time in works and more time on the road. Although the 'Q1's' cylinders and wheel diameters were the same as Maunsell's 'Q' class, the Bulleid engines with their higher boiler pressure and larger firebox were as different in performance as they were in appearance.

Below:
Probably the last 0-6-0 tender engine built in Great Britain for a British railway: Bulleid 'Q1' 0-6-0 No 33040 runs on to Nine Elms Shed, where she was ultimately stored following withdrawal in June 1964, pending scrapping. *Author*

Today, almost 20 years since the end of BR steam, there has been a subtle but discernible change in attitudes towards different classes of locomotives, and the 'Q1' is undoubtedly a beneficiary, in retrospect, of some admiration. As Britain's last new design of 0-6-0, built in wartime to austerity specifications, it is fair to say that the 'Q1' was more *distinctive* than any of the BR Standard designs, all of which had leading bogies of two or four wheels. Indeed, offhand I cannot think of any new postwar design of steam engine, worldwide, that featured either an 0-6-0 wheel-arrangement or indeed an engine without a leading truck or bogie. If I am failing in memory or knowledge someone will undoubtedly tell me.

Even as late as 1962, at the end of which year my photo mission commenced, there was still an immense variety of 0-6-0 tender locomotives at work in Britain. They spanned the generations, and in terms of long-lived wheel-arrangements probably hold the record. From the earliest days of steam, through the Railway Mania, into the 20th century and World War 2, the 0-6-0 held sway. From Matthew Kirtley to O. V. S. Bulleid, from Gooch to Gresley, north, south, east and west, the 0-6-0 was universally deployed. Indeed, at the turn of the

century more than one third of the 20,000 locomotives in service on Britain's railways were 0-6-0 tender types. When first my faithful Voigtlander was aimed at a steam engine, many Pre-Grouping and not a few Victorian locomotives were still at work, from Caithness to Cornwall.

The first 0-6-0 that I photographed in December 1962, was Collett '2251' class No 2219 inside the diminutive engine shed at Highbridge, on the Somerset & Dorset. At the time my ignorance of motive power matters and of railway history did not immediately impress upon me the significance of a GWR locomotive on what had until very recently

---

Below:
With endless permutations of 0-6-0s the Midland Railway provides profuse examples for inclusion in this chapter. Arbitrarily my choice fell on this photograph of a standard Johnson goods engine, No 1374, at Lancaster shed c1903-6. Many of these locomotives, albeit bewilderingly rebuilt and reboilered from time to time by MR, LMS and BR, ran for more than three-quarters of a century. 1374 was built by Dubs in May 1878, and withdrawn by BR in November 1958.

Left:
Good fortune alone enabled me to capture on colour film Maunsell 'Q' 0-6-0 No 30549, with stovepipe chimney, on shed at Redhill in April 1963. That chimney utterly transforms the appearance of what is the penultimate class of 0-6-0 designed and built by a British railway. Notwithstanding the technical reasons, it has to me always seemed odd that Bulleid's 'Q1' was designated thus, as its external appearance (not least the 5ft 1in wheels) could have hardly looked more different from Maunsell's 'Q'.

Top:
Feltham (70B) plays host to 'Q1' 0-6-0 No 33026 on a bright June day in 1964. Lack of 'colour' highlights the problem created by filthy locomotives in drab surroundings, but Bulleid's BFB wheels are well in evidence here.

Above:
Longevity was, of course, a great tribute both to design and to quality. In the North-East, the 'J27' 0-6-0 freight engines were introduced on to the North Eastern Railway (NER) as long ago as 1906, yet at least eight had survived into the winter of 1965/66. The flavour of the railway scene on Tyneside is represented by the impressive track layout at Newcastle Central, which is approached by 'J27' No 65805 on 5 August 1965 as it threads the crossovers, to pass through the great station with a brake van. The poor quality of this photograph highlights the paucity of my North-Eastern material.

been the preserve of Derby machines. Indeed, whilst bowing to no-one in my affection for the S&D, it cannot be said that these Collett 0-6-0s seemed out of place on 'The Branch' of the S&D, at least not to someone who had missed the Johnson '3Fs'.

The following month was one of the worst on record, certainly since the winter of 1947. In snow, fog and ice, steam kept the railways going. During some hours of frigid vigil on Bristol Temple Meads station, my first sighting of an LMS '4F' 0-6-0 produced a photograph of No 44269 running 'light engine' under the girder bridge to the south of the station. These superheater engines were still in service over many of the former LMS lines. With their appearance bearing such similarity to their Fowler forebears, they appealed to me as a very recent re-entrant to railway observation, notwithstanding that, to the experienced eye, they were one of the most common examples of a most unremarkable locomotive type.

My first camera-sighting of an 0-6-0, as previously mentioned, was '2251' class No 2219 at Highbridge: the last was 'J36' No 65234 at Edinburgh St Margarets Shed, on 5 August 1965, although by this date it was motionless in its duty as a stationary boiler. In fact it was earlier that same day, when my lens captured 'J27' No 65805 at Newcastle Central, that I photographed my last 0-6-0 in active service with British Rail. This was both the first and last time that I saw a 'J27', nearly 60 years since the introduction of the class by William Worsdell on the North Eastern Railway: a good example of the longevity that characterised the type on Britain's railway system.

In spite of the large numbers and long life of 0-6-0s on our railways, they were in retreat by the time I started my photography in November 1962. The classes that I was able to see between then and the end of steam were as follows:

MR	LSWR	NER	SR
Johnson '3F'	'700'	'J27'	'Q'
Fowler '4F'			'Q1'
NBR	GWR	LMS	
'J36'	'2251'	'4F'	

Perhaps of all strands of tender locomotive genealogy, the Midland and LMS 0-6-0 engines spanned the greatest period of years. Indeed the Midland, with its voluminous mineral traffic, had about 1000 0-6-0 tender engines, which continued to bear the brunt of its freight traffic until the end of that railway's independent existence.

More ancient than the '4F' were the Midland '3F' 0-6-0s, some of which still performed revenue-earning tasks into the 1960s. On a visit to Bedford in April 1963, I found No 43453 dead at the back of the shed. With the connivance of the foreman, 'Black Five' No 45416 dragged the veteran into the daylight for my camera.

With West Coast main line electrification, most of the remaining Midland and LMS '4F' 0-6-0s were to be found north of Crewe. Warrington Dallam had its share, all by 1965 sporting the diagonal yellow cabside stripe; No 44063 had steam to spare outside the shed on 23 April 1964. The day before, I photographed one of the Fowler Midland engines at Clifton Junction; and a Nottingham (16A) shedplate was displayed by No 43865, at Willesden on 5 July. That year I saw LMS '4Fs' at Bristol Barrow Road, at Peak Forest, at Newton Heath and again at Dallam in December. Their end was nigh.

With opportunities to travel around the country, always with my camera, there was no logic in the sequence of sightings of either class or ages of locomotives, so I must rely on memory and record to put some semblance into these chapters. My reference to photographing that Holmes' North British 'C' class — later LNER Class J36 — No 65234, albeit as stationary boiler, at Edinburgh St Margarets on 5 August 1965, reminds me that this is one of the few classes of 0-6-0 of which some were dignified by being named. Twenty-five of these NB engines commemorated their service in France during World War 1 by receiving names, most of which were associated with the conflict. Oddly an unnamed 'J36', No 65311, had the name *Haig* unofficially painted on during summer 1953. It remained thus adorned for two years, entered Inverurie Works for overhaul and emerged with the name 'officially' attached. Thus No 65311 was distinguished by being the last 0-6-0 to be named on Britain's railways — at least in the BR steam era.

In spite of — or indeed because of — the very large number of locomotives of this wheel-arrangement, it was only really towards the end of steam that photographers took much notice of the ubiquitous 0-6-0. Yet for my part, I sought them out. From my Bedford adventure with the '3F', I went on to Wellingborough and photographed another Johnson '3F' and a Midland '4F', both dead inside the roundhouse. It seems that my photography commenced almost coincidentally with the demise of the 0-6-0. On 18 May 1963 I visited Eastleigh where a member of another extinct Victorian class was awaiting scrapping — this time No 30346, one of Drummond's LSWR '700' class, known as 'Black Motors'. That was a day of rare sightings for me — but all, sadly, had dropped their fires for the last time.

To detail all my photographs would be tedious in the extreme, be it of 0-6-0 or any other wheel-arrangement. The 0-6-0 was undoubtedly the workhorse of Britain's railways. The Pacifics had the image of glamour, the Panniers and 'Jinties' the ubiquitous ebullience; there were types and classes famed for innovation, style and speed; the 0-6-0 has really no memorial, but to true enthusiasts its worth will be neither undervalued nor forgotten.

CHAPTER THREE

TEN-COUPLED

Sheer size has never been the British answer to mechanical or indeed behavioural matters. Indeed one of the attributes of our nation is a degree of shyness and inhibition that differentiates us from, shall we say, our North American cousins. Where they epitomise size, noise and extravagance, we tend towards the modest, quiet and workmanlike. If this is true in matters of character, it is certainly true too in relation to motive power in the steam era. The sheer bulk of those grotesque machines epitomised by 'Big Boy', articulation and multi-bogied wheel-arrangements, left me quite cold and disinterested.

Perhaps it was therefore only when this national shyness and modesty was confronted by the exigencies of war that, with the solitary exception of the unique Great Eastern 'Decapod' of 1902, and of 'Big Bertha' on the Lickey Incline, the first ten-coupled locomotives were built for Britain's railways. Indeed it has to be said that these locomotives — the Riddles WD 'Austerity' 2-10-0s — were in fact built neither for extra power nor indeed mainly for use in Britain. They were built by the North British Locomotive Company (NBL) to Robin Riddles' design, with the specific intention to produce a locomotive with both wider route availability and the necessarily lighter axle-loading, but with the job specification of fulfilling similar tasks to his 'Austerity' 2-8-0. Thus it was working conditions, track and environment, rather than the need for greater power that produced the demand for the 2-10-0 wheel-arrangement. Indeed, the tractive effort of the 2-8-0 and the 2-10-0 were the same.

The axle-loading on the 'Austerity' 2-10-0 was 13½ tons as opposed to the 15½ tons of the 2-8-0. The size, number and arrangement of wheels on a steam locomotive are determined by various factors, including the length and weight of the engine; the permitted axle load on the lines over which it will run, as well as their gradients and curves; and the weight of trains it will have to haul. Thus Riddles plumped for 2-10-0 rather than the 2-8-2 which was his initial reaction to the War Department requirement of a derivative of his 2-8-0. The extra pair of coupled wheels enabled him to specify a larger boiler and still provide the lighter axle loading. To add to the locomotive's manoeuvrability he decided to provide flangeless centre-coupled wheels and flanges of reduced thickness on the wheels on either side of the centre one.

The first of Riddles' 2-10-0s emerged from the NBL works in June 1944. The first 20 of the total of 150 engines built by NBL were sent to the Middle East. I never saw one in steam, but in Greece, in 1983, my reward for giving up three days on the beach in Halkidiki was to find a few of these fine engines dumped in one of the three steam graveyards in Thessaloniki.

Fine engines they were, too. Indeed, no less an authority than Colonel H. C. B. Rogers has described them as 'unquestionably one of the masterpieces of British locomotive design'.

That the 'Austerity' 2-10-0 was British built for use mainly overseas, and that many saw service in the Middle East, enables me to justify the inclusion here of a few sentences both on other British-built ten-coupled engines designed for overseas customers; and on the few foreign-built ten-coupled machines that I have seen and photographed in the last few years.

Readers of my railway books will know that I have no pretensions to professional status, either as photographer or historian. My travels have taken me to China on a number of occasions, and the Chinese 'QJ' 2-10-2 is an impressive machine, about which I wrote a chapter in *To China for Steam*. Derived from the Russian 'LV' class of the same wheel-arrangement, the 'QJ' is still in production and is *per se*, the final production manifestation of the steam locomotive engineer.

In addition to the 'QJ' 2-10-2 with its cylinders, coupled wheels and valve-gear derived from the Soviet 'LV' class, China took delivery of about 1,250 Russian 'FD' class 2-10-2s in the late 1950s and early 1960s. With the change in relations between the two nations, these locomotives were being withdrawn perhaps earlier than they might have been, and even in 1982 they were quite hard to find, although I captured one on shed — if that is the word for the open-air servicing facilities — at Luoyang.

Whilst China's ten-coupled motive power has no direct British ancestry, India still provides a working environment for the products of many of the great British locomotive manufacturers, including the North British Locomotive Company, sadly no longer building engines for export around the globe. One can only speculate about the fate of one of their early ten-coupled machines, a class of 2-10-0 built for the Great Indian Peninsular Railway and introduced in 1919. Unsurprisingly these engines and their contemporaries from Vulcan Foundry and Beyer Peacock, all had a distinctively 'British' appearance, although this 2-10-0 was some years ahead of anything similar running on British metals.

As I write these words, amongst my recent working steam railway photography has been some in that troubled and unhappy country, South Africa. Eight-coupled motive-power is the order of the day on their 3ft 6in gauge, and some British-built machines are still at work, although for how much longer is not too certain. No mention was made of an experimental 2-10-4 built by North British in 1937 for use on track laid with 60lb rail. Equipped with a mechanical stoker, the engine alone weighed 171 tons, and its boiler was interchangeable with the '15E' and '15F' classes of 4-8-2, examples of which I was fortunate enough to see and photograph, the former being introduced on South African railways in 1935; notwithstanding the fact that the '15Es' were built by Robert Stephenson & Co, by Henschel and by Berliner Maschinenbau, whilst the '15Fs' were built by the latter two German manufacturers as well as by North British and by Beyer Peacock. As with Riddles' 'Austerity' 2-10-0, the NBL 2-10-4 had some flangeless driving wheels. Furthermore, its self-cleaning screens in the smokebox were a precursor to similar practice adopted years later as standard by British Railways. Incidentally, still at work in 1985, at Germiston, Johannesburg, were a handful of North British 0-8-0 shunting locomotives.

The link between British-built ten-coupled locomotives, non-British-built machines and my travels excuses my mentioning another class of 2-10-0 built by Beyer Peacock for the Turkish State Railways (TCDD) in 1964. In this instance, these were a derivative of a German design, previously acquired by the Turkish railways from several manufacturers. Fitted with Westinghouse brake equipment, these imposing machines developed a nominal tractive effort of 57,560lb at 85% boiler pressure.

Some of Riddles' 'Austerity' 2-10-0s found their way to Turkey, but the TCDD was a better customer for German rather than British equipment. Large numbers of 'Kriegslok' 2-10-0s saw service on TCDD, some of them still in service at the time of writing, and kept in excellent condition.

During this brief soliloquy on overseas ten-coupled locomotives, I mentioned that my most recent working steam railway photography had been in South Africa. Since then a brief look at the (steam-less) railways of Thailand caused me to study their railway and locomotive history; and a strange tale it is, with conversion of the main, northern line from Bangkok, from standard gauge to metre gauge in the 1920s. The only point of mentioning this is to relate the fact that the last standard gauge engines built for the Thai railway system were two 0-10-0 tender locomotives supplied by Hanomag in 1913.

Having digressed as far afield as China, India, South Africa and Turkey it is time to remind myself that the primary purpose of this book is to feature British steam locomotives. It is obviously the paucity of ten-coupled classes that has caused my digression, and my failure yet to mention the most obvious, most numerous, most recent, most successful, most versatile — and in my case most often seen — example of 'British ten-coupled', namely the BR Standard '9F' 2-10-0. Before eulogising this outstanding engine, relating it to its immediate precursor by the same designer, namely the WD 'Austerity' 2-10-0, mention must be made of the only other ten-coupled locomotive to run on British metals between the Great Eastern 'Decapod' and Riddles' 'Austerity', namely the Midland 0-10-0 Lickey Incline banking engine, still at work when the 'Austerities' entered service.

In the long saga of British steam locomotive history, few individual locomotives were designed and built as a class of one. The 'Decapod' was purely an experimental engine, designed by James Holden and built in 1902. Nothing quite like it was seen before or has been seen since on any British railway. With an enormous boiler, and a firebox extending to the full width of the frame; with the water carried in a well-tank beneath the bunker, the 'Decapod' was almost certainly the most powerful locomotive in the world at the time. As on her later ten-coupled sisters, the middle pair of driving wheels were flangeless.

The purpose for which the 'Decapod' was built, was to ascertain the capabilities of steam haulage, vis-à-vis electric traction, for the Great Eastern's suburban services from Liverpool Street, acceleration being the acid-test of comparability, with stand-to-30mph in 30sec with a train in excess of 300 tons being the parameter. To the surprise and doubtless consternation of the electro-fanatics, the 'Decapod', with a train of 335 tons, exceeded this target on her tests; and consequently Great Eastern electrification plans were shelved — for decades. Not

Above:

One of the 10 Crosti-boilered '9F' 2-10-0s, No 92024, takes water on Birkenhead shed, on 4 July 1965. Notwithstanding reconversion to normal, there was no mistaking the ex-Crosti engines, as is self-evident. The 12A shedplate indicates a Carlisle Kingmoor engine — presumably recently out-shopped and unlikely to remain clean for long.

Below:

Officially due to close in three months' time, Izmir Alcançak's small remaining stud of steam locomotives were nevertheless, by September 1985, in a very different state from their British counterparts in steam's twilight. The wheel balances and motion cut a colourful dash when compared with our '9Fs'. German Kriegslok 'Austerity' 2-10-0, No 56514, built by Borsig in 1943 (DRB '52' class), poses in the afternoon sun.

surprisingly, however, the weight of the locomotive would have necessitated considerable strengthening of track and bridges. This, combined with permanent way restrictions, resulted in stalemate. 'Decapod' was years ahead of her time. In 1906 the engine was rebuilt as an 0-8-0 tender locomotive for freight use, but as an unique unit of motive-power her days were numbered, and Britain's first ten-coupled engine was finally scrapped in 1913. Her 'memento' however, in that she beat off the challenge of electrification, was to be the stalking horse for what became, in 1922, the most intensive steam-operated suburban service in the world.

Doubtless the 'Decapod' was the sensation of her day, in an era when experimentation in steam locomotive power was the natural expression of the rivalry and competitiveness of the Pre-Grouping companies. Phrases such as 'pushing materials beyond the limits of known technology' had not been invented, and would have been merely an additional challenge to Chief Mechanical Engineers, whose new ideas had to be tested, not in some laboratory, but at the platform's edge. James Holden — or to be more precise his Chief Draughtsman at Stratford, F. V. Russell — was responding to the challenge of electrification by pushing the performance frontiers of steam motive power beyond its contemporary proven capacity for quick acceleration with a heavy load.

As I rummaged around the library of the Institution of Mechanical Engineers whilst assembling material for this book, the ghosts of the great men of the steam era seemed all around. James Holden gave his audience information on the results of the 'Decapod' experiment, in a lecture at the IMechE in March 1906. His contribution followed the presentation of a paper by G. J. Churchward. As I searched for information on the subject of locomotive wheels one thought, inevitably, of O. V. S. Bulleid, his wheels and his 'Leader' class locomotive; the latter lies outside the scope of this chapter or indeed this book, but was surely the manifestation of challenge and experimentation to meet the demands of the traveller of the day, to which Russell and Holden responded in the shape of that amazing, original and for me utterly intriguing machine, the 'Decapod'.

Seventeen years elapsed between the construction of the first and second ten-coupled British steam locomotive. Whilst the Great Eastern 'Decapod' is a fantasy from the past, the Midland Railway's entry into the realms of the ten-coupled locomotive is much more within the living memory. Indeed, on Friday 9 May 1980 I rode in the cab of a diesel locomotive driven, between Westbury and Portsmouth, by Michael Richardson, who had himself fired this famous locomotive — the Lickey Banker, known to countless railwaymen and enthusiasts as 'Big Bertha'. Originally numbered 2290 by the Midland Railway, she was renumbered 22290 by the

LMS in 1947, and 58100 by BR the following year.

If 'Big Bertha's' number varied, her duties certainly did not. Rarely has a single British locomotive clocked up such a mileage but been virtually nowhere: of the 838,856 miles run, the vast majority were accumulated up and down the two miles of the Lickey Incline between Bromsgrove and Blackwell, on the main line of the former Midland Railway's route between Bristol and Birmingham. The only other journey undertaken was the occasional run to Derby for overhaul, although in July 1924 she carried out a test run from Wellingborough to Brent as part of the experimentation on the Toton-Brent coal trains. E. S. Cox, recalling his delight on being designated one of the crew for this test, was less than enthusiastic about the outcome; writing in *Locomotive Panorama* he says: 'Over the performance itself it is best to draw a veil. No record appears to remain but memory recalls that it was agreed by common consent that the engine was not, repeat not, suitable for working this kind of traffic.' Back to Bromsgrove went 'Big Bertha'.

Derby was, of course, 'Big Bertha's' birthplace. The Lickey Incline in steam days was always a formidable obstacle in the face of northbound trains on this busy main line, and virtually every train required banking assistance on the 1 in 37½ gradient. For generations the Midland Railway kept a stud of 0-6-0 tank engines on shed at Bromsgrove with which to undertake this task. 'Big Bertha', by far the largest and heaviest locomotive ever built by the Midland Railway, with its small-engine policy, was designed to cope with the work of two 0-6-0 tanks. She was a qualified success, vindicating Derby's decision, although she herself was not infrequently assisted in her banking duties. Not every driver on northbound trains arriving at Bromsgrove would share the eulogies. Indeed, O. S. Nock, reporting on a visit to the Lickey in 1949, recalls that 'the boiler could not produce enough steam to sustain an all-out effort for the 8min of the ascent, banking a passenger train'. He goes on to relate how the boiler pressure dropped from 180lb at the bottom of the incline, to 135lb on passing Blackwell, and reports that, on his footplate experiences over the years, many drivers expressed the preference for two 0-6-0T bankers, to the solo effort of 'Big Bertha'. Such is the conflict between romance and reality; but 'Big Bertha' would surely not have survived from 1919 to 1956 unless she was reasonably competent to carry out a vital task on a key trunk route.

Brian Haresnape, in his excellent *Fowler Locomotives* — one of a series of railway books — details the varied proposals which emerged from Derby with which to tackle the Lickey problem, one of which was a 2-10-0. It was to be a quarter of a century later that the first British locomotive of such a wheel-arrangement was to appear on the scene, in the shape of the Riddles WD 'Austerity'. Perhaps

Above:
Britain's first ten-coupled locomotive, the Great Eastern 'Decapod'. Its success in achieving acceleration targets thwarted the ambitions of the electrification enthusiasts, and led to the creation of the 'Jazz' trains, the most intensive steam-hauled suburban services in the world. The only 0-10-0 tank engine ever to run in Britain, this picture has been seen before, as few photographs exist of this one-off curiosity, which remains an item of fascination for railway historians and enthusiasts.

not altogether surprisingly, however, it was another Riddles 2-10-0, his BR Standard '9F', that finally supplanted 'Big Bertha' at Bromsgrove when the unique 0-10-0 tender locomotive — the only one ever to run on Britain's railway system — was withdrawn in 1956.

How desperately sad that the remarkable and long-lived 'Big Bertha' — let alone the Great Eastern 'Decapod' — did not survive into the ranks of preserved locomotives. However, before passing on to the next of the quartet of British decapods, I feel bound to mention my one and only visit to the Lickey. It was an indescribably foul 'Summer' day, 6 June 1964. The '9Fs' had replaced 'Big Bertha' nearly 10 years previously, and were clearly tackling their task with complete competence. Through the driving incessant rain, which created cascading rivers on either side of the track down the Incline, the Riddles 2-10-0s pounded up the grade, but they were not alone. By a quirk of fate so quintessentially piquant for students of railway history, it was Great Western '94xx' 0-6-0 Pannier tanks, rather than their Midland/LMS rivals, that shared the banking duties on the Lickey at the end of steam. Of all the battles fought out between the great Pre-Grouping companies in the formative years in the middle of the 19th century, the loss by the GWR to the Midland of the main line between Bristol and Birmingham was probably the most serious. But, as elsewhere — notably west of Salisbury on the lines of the former London and South Western Railway — the ghosts of the directors of the GWR had the last laugh over their erstwhile rivals.

According to my notes of that wet and dismal day now nearly a quarter of a century ago we (for I was accompanied by another damp but determined enthusiast, Ed Chilton, then managing director of Rank Xerox) saw, or at least I certainly photo-graphed, three '9Fs' — Nos 92083/230, plus one that remains unidentified. Of the Pannier tanks, numbers 8400/2 and 9493 were captured for posterity.

Interestingly, one freight, hauled by a GWR 'Hall' 4-6-0, was banked by a '9F' and a '94xx' Pannier tank. I do not know if 'Big Bertha' herself was often, rarely or ever assisted in her banking tasks by other locomotives. How did those responsible for such decisions themselves regard the Midland 0-10-0? Would it have been considered a loss of face to have to provide additional banking assistance to the big engine? I cannot recall ever reading or hearing about such an esoteric point.

In digressing about that day on Lickey my attention has been somewhat diverted from the task in hand, namely, that of writing about ten-coupled locomotives. I do not know whether any of the Riddles 'Austerity' 2-10-0s — the third in the list of the only four British ten-coupled locomotive classes — ever tackled Lickey. Strange it is however, and indicative of changing eras, that the numbers comprising the four different classes were 1:1:150*:251 respectively. Perhaps this is the relevant place in this chapter, in which to tabulate some of the details of the four ten-coupled types.

*Although 150 WD 2-10-0s were built, only 25 were used on BR.

Visiting Feltham from Leicester Midland (15A) on 3 October 1964, is '9F' No 92123, the autumn sunshine illuminating the 5ft 0in driving wheels. On the last class of British steam locomotive to be built, those small wheels perhaps finally proved the point that 8ft diameter was not a concomitant of fast running. No 92123 was transferred away from Leicester to Birkenhead in April 1965, and was allocated to Birkenhead at the same time that I was 'on duty' there as Prospective Parliamentary Candidate.

Another British-built, Riddles-designed ten-coupled locomotive, but this time far from Birkenhead. WD 'Austerity'. 2-10-0, Hellenic State Railway Class L6 No 966, rusts away in a corner of a foreign field, at Thessaloniki, on 2 September 1983. Sixteen of these North British-built engines went to Egypt in 1944, some years thereafter being acquired by the Greeks. Compare the outline seen here with the 'WD' 2-8-0 on page 97.

Locomotive	Date introduced & designer	Wheel-arrangement	Railway	Numbers built	Driving wheels	Cylinders	Boiler pressure	Weight (locomotive)	Tractive effort @85% (lb)	Comments
'Decapod'	1902 J. Holden	0-10-0T	Great Eastern	1	4ft 6in	(3) 18½in×24in	200lb	80 tons	43,000	Probably world's most powerful locomotive
Lickey Banker	1919 H. Fowler	0-10-0	Midland	1	4ft 7½in	(4) 16¾in×28in	180lb	74 tons (approx)	43,312	Fitted with headlight and used on the Lickey Incline Nickname: *Big Bertha*
WD 'Austerity'	1943 R. A. Riddles	2-10-0	War Department	150	4ft 8½in	(2) 19in×28in	225lb	78.6 tons	34,215	Only 25 ran in BR service
'9F'	1954 R. A. Riddles	2-10-0	BR	251	5ft	(2) 20in×28in	250lb	86.7 tons	39,667	Crosti-boilered engines had different details

Having mentioned the two 'one-offs', it is time to turn to the remaining two ten-coupled types. If 1902 was still in the era of the grand railway experiment, and 1919 saw the postwar re-establishment of the identities of the railway companies, then 1943 was a different time indeed. The tide of World War 2 was on the turn. The Allied plans for the invasion of occupied Europe were taking shape. Utilitarianism and functionality rather than flamboyance and speciality were the order of the day. As mentioned earlier in this chapter, Robin Riddles was charged with the task of designing and having built a class of locomotive that would effectively pull as great a weight as possible, as far as possible, as often as possible, on track that was likely to be of very poor quality, probably a long distance from full and adequate repair and even maintenance facilities. The War Department (WD) 'Austerity' 2-8-0 immediately earned itself a well-justified reputation for all these attributes: and the 2-10-0 was therefore a derivative of a proven machine, with even wider route availability. Perhaps not surprisingly, therefore, the WD 2-10-0 attracted comparatively little attention — certainly less than its two single ten-coupled predecessors. Indeed, the most often attributed feature of this splendid locomotive was as the derived child of its designer's own 2-8-0, or as the precursor of the same designer's '9F' 2-10-0. Before we turn to the '9F', however, let us spare a moment for the WD 2-10-0.

Bearing in mind the design criteria for these locomotives, they seem to have been overlooked in the interest taken in them as compared to their near-contemporaries. Indeed, in the various tests carried out in the early years of nationalisation, they were criticised on numerous counts when compared to the Stanier '8F', GWR '28xx' and LNER 'O1' 2-8-0s. Yet for all these criticisms it seems that, for those sheds to which they were allocated, the WD 2-8-0 and 2-10-0 locomotives were truly appreciated. Thoroughbreds visually they were not; but for the sheer grinding donkey-work that was their daily lot, those responsible for clearing the marshalling yards and keeping the show on the road, knew a good workhorse when they saw one — theoretical tests be damned.

Whilst Riddles' 2-8-0 was based on the Stanier '8F', the 2-10-0 was his own conception, and the wide firebox was designed to cope with the lack of good fuel on the continent during the latter days of World War 2 — a situation not unknown in Britain either. The 2-8-0s had shown a refusal to steam on French, Dutch and Belgian fuel.

Of the 150 2-10-0s turned out by the North British Locomotive Co — of which one, No 73755, became the 1,000th WD locomotive built in Britain and ferried to Europe — 103 were loaned to the Netherlands Railway during 1945/6. The movement and location of these engines makes interesting reading and is fairly well documented. When built they were put to work on Britain's railways prior to shipment overseas to further the war effort. With the speed of the Allied advance, 27 of the big engines never left these shores, 20 on the LNER and seven remaining in the hands of the War Department for their own use. Ultimately the 20 engines on the LNER plus five of the seven originally in WD ownership were purchased by and taken into BR stock in 1948, and in due course were numbered 90750-90774. In fact the 20 engines which the LNER had received directly from North British in 1945 had been in store prior to their purchase by BR: and two of the five which went to BR from the War Department had actually been transferred to the LMS from the WD's Cairnryan Military Railway. The remaining three, making up the BR total of 25, came from Longmoor and apparently had never even been steamed. When one thinks of the number of people taking railway photographs between 1948 and 1962, it is surprising how comparatively few pictures of these 2-10-0s have been published. With the two exceptions of the Great Eastern 'Decapod' and the Midland Lickey Banker, no ten-coupled locomotive had ever run on British metals: and the two forebears had been restricted to such a tightly-defined area that they can barely be accounted for as reasonable camera targets. As mentioned previously, these Riddles locomotives will have seemed to many people as merely on the one hand an extension of his 2-8-0; and on the other the precursor of his '9F'; thus photographically they seem to have failed to enthuse the cameramen of their day. Add to this the disdain felt by many people towards the 'Austerities' and one has, I suppose, the reason for the paucity of material. Perhaps somebody will publish a book to prove me wrong.

Thanks to the laborious work of Peter Hands, one can now trace the precise whereabouts of most of the locomotives on British Rail's books from 1957 until the end of steam. From the records it transpires that the 25 'Austerity' 2-10-0s spent most of their working BR lives in Scotland. In January 1957 they were allocated as follows:

90750/2/4/6/8/60/ 1/2/4/6/70/1/2	66B	Motherwell
90751/67	66A	Polmadie (Glasgow)
90753/68	64D	Carstairs
90755/7/9/65/73/4	65F	Grangemouth
90763	68A	Kingmoor (Carlisle)

With the exception of No 90763, all remained on the Scottish Region for the duration of their time: as a class they were remarkably stable in their location, which presumably indicates satisfactory service.

On 23 February 1958, Carlisle Kingmoor MPD changed its shedcode from 68A to 12A on its transfer from Scottish to London Midland Region control; No 90763 was thus the sole escapee. In August 1959 she was transferred away south to Bidston for 12 months, only to return to Kingmoor in July 1960. The entire class was withdrawn between July 1961 (90753/4 from Carstairs and Motherwell respectively) and December 1962 when 17 went, clearly as a matter of policy rather than as a result of condition. This situation was sadly to become a familiar one with the wanton destruction of hordes of locomotives with decades of service left in them.

None of the BR 'Austerity' 2-10-0s survived into preservation, although one of the War Department engines did, and lives today in the good care of the Severn Valley Railway. Furthermore, two more of the NB engines, which survived their service in Greece after varied careers, have been shipped back to Britain for restoration to working order. The one on the Mid-Hants Railway has been magnificently 'restored' to BR condition and numbered 90775, to create the illusion of being the 26th BR 'Austerity' 2-10-0, to follow the 25 which were numbered 90750-74. The other awaits restoration on the North Yorkshire Moors Railway at the time of writing.

Only now, all these years after the demise of the ten-coupled 'Austerities', are these engines finding friends who care enough to bestow upon them the interest and merit they undoubtedly deserve. Thanks only to their ability to survive the running conditions, maintenance and service facilities and the variation in driving and firing techniques they encountered in a number of countries, not all of which are renowned for mechanical excellence, have a handful survived, to be returned as prodigals to the land of their birth.

Whatever disinterest may have seemed to surround Robin Riddles' first 2-10-0, it was certainly not mirrored in his second machine of this wheel-arrangement. Six years after British Railways' purchase of the 25 'Austerities', came the introduction of the last of the new BR Standard steam locomotive classes. There are many commentators more learned than I — indeed, there are few less so — and most will say that BR's last was also the best. Indeed, the tragedy, for it was no less than that, is that these magnificent locomotives were never allowed to complete their useful revenue-earning lives. That the last '9F', named *Evening Star* and appropriately built at Swindon, entered service a mere four years before the first members of the class were withdrawn, is one of the most grotesque pieces of wastefulness perpetrated by any nationalised industry.

To write anything original about the '9Fs', would strain both my research facilities and indeed my imagination. Brian Haresnape has described *Evening Star* as 'the most famous freight engine of all time', although the 'Jones Goods' must in its day have created as much interest, albeit amongst a much more restricted audience. As the '9Fs' were spread throughout the BR System it became clear, however, that this was no mere 'freight engine'. Regretfully, their lack of steam heating facilities; their late arrival on the scene; the time taken fully to appreciate their potential as passenger locomotives; and the compression in time between their introduction and steam's elimination, meant that there was no sustained attempt to modify, develop and test these magnificent machines to what would undoubtedly have been their full potential.

Anyone who has seen the Chinese 'QJ' class 2-10-2 at work on long-distance passenger trains, realises the way in which time has overtaken the perceived wisdom of the early years of steam, when large diameter wheels were equated with speed. For those who followed the life of the '9Fs', perhaps the most surprising was the discovery, late in their lives and at British steam's last gasp, of the suitability and speed potential of these remarkable engines, with their 5ft-diameter coupled wheels: a long way indeed from the 'Seven-Foot Singles' of the early years.

Much has been written over the past 30 years about the '9F'. As the last class of steam locomotive to enter service, it could expect to be subject to close scrutiny. Indeed, had E. S. Cox and his committee of Chief Draughtsmen had their way it would probably never have been built. These gentlemen, conservative to the end, wanted a 2-8-2 with the 'Britannia' boiler and 5ft 3in coupled wheels. A memorandum was circulated setting out 10 good reasons why a 2-10-0 was not suitable: but Robin Riddles, at whom these arguments were aimed, persisted. The requirement for an engine to handle heavy fast freight was, he believed, more likely to be fulfilled with a ten-coupled locomotive without trailing wheels, than by an eight-coupled machine with them. Without myself attempting to tackle technical explanations, he contended that a steam locomotive, when starting off or when pulling slowly up a heavy gradient, tends to 'sit back' on its trailing wheels, thus transferring some of its adhesive weight to those wheels. Clearly, if those trailing wheels are uncoupled and 'inactive' the locomotive will suffer loss of adhesion. That is why Pacifics tend to slip more on starting than does a 4-6-0. A 2-8-2 would have less adhesion, on starting, than a 2-8-0. As the need was for a heavy freight locomotive capable of good acceleration from standing starts, plus a good turn of speed; and as Riddles was both the man in charge and the man responsible for the 'Austerity' 2-8-0 and 2-10-0, his influence prevailed, and the '9F' was born.

It was not long after their introduction that they began to show their unexpected talent as fast, smooth and safe runners on express passenger duty. They began to acquire an enviable reputation not only for versatility but also for reliability. Shed-masters faced with rostering motive power for summer specials and long-distance excursions found a new friend. On the old Great Central they were even rostered for regular work on express passenger trains such as the 'Master Cutler' and the 'South Yorkshireman'. Very briefly they headed the 'Capitals United' between Cardiff and Paddington. However, such enthusiastic use of a locomotive designed for less sustained speed work caused unacceptably high wear in the cylinders and other running gear, with consequentially reduced periods between overhaul resulting from what, in reality, was misuse; in 1959 a decree was issued from headquarters to desist from using the '9Fs' on regular passenger work. An exception was made on the Somerset & Dorset (S&D), where their performance is now part of the folklore both of this line and of the engines themselves. There is nothing I could or would add to the immortal words and pictures of Ivo Peters.

I have mentioned the role of the '9Fs' as Lickey Bankers. Other tough duties for which they became a legend in their own lifetime were the Consett iron-ore trains from the Tyne Dock Staithes to the furnaces of the Consett Iron Company and the Long Meg-Widnes Anhydrite trains over the Settle & Carlisle. On the S&D the maximum passenger load without a pilot had been eight bogies for a Class 5; and the same for Bulleid Light Pacifics, which were prone to serious slipping. The S&D '7F' 2-8-0s, with their good adhesion, were on occasion allowed to take 10 bogies at a pinch: the '9Fs' were regularly rostered for 12. The S&D was not the only cross-country route on which the '9Fs' performed prodigious feats. Less publicised, but equally impressive, was their work on the Fawley-Bromford Bridge oil tank trains running over the Didcot, Newbury & Southampton line, thrice daily with a 1,200-ton load. For this task six '9Fs' were allocated

to Eastleigh shed. With typical British pessimism, the pundits there predicted trouble on the lengthy single-line sections, much of it graded at 1 : 106. These fears soon proved groundless.

Tales of individual exploits by '9Fs' are legion, and some of the more delightful ones are recounted by Colonel H. C. B. Rogers in his excellent book *Riddles and the '9Fs'*. His opening sentence to Chapter 4 says it all — 'Riddles' Standard "9Fs" must constitute one of the very few classes of locomotives which have been free from any criticism of substance'.

The only major experiment, carried out on 10 of the '9Fs', was the fitting of a Crosti boiler. Again with apologies to anyone technically-minded who may by chance read this, my amateur's explanation thereof, is of a system intended to save fuel consumption by utilising the heat which, in a conventional steam locomotive, is wasted into the air through the chimney. The contract between BR and the Italian Franco company related the latter's earnings to the former's savings; but unfortunately the resultant tests produced very disappointing savings. The preheater drums were removed, and the crews on the Crosti-boilered engines were released from the discomfort of swirling smoke and steam all round the footplate. The ten engines, numbers 92020-92029, were altered back to 'normal' design, though they retained the smaller-diameter boilers and a distinctive appearance (see page 45) They remained non-standard in dimension and specification.

This chapter has become rather long; let me conclude with my own sounds, sights and memories of a memorable locomotive, which we can still occasionally enjoy with David Shepherd's *Black Prince* No 92203 at Cranmore on the East Somerset Railway, or of course, No 92220, *Evening Star*. Other '9Fs' which languished at Woodhams, Barry, and which 'escaped' therefrom may yet feel fire again too; that is for the future. For me, rekindled railway interest and enthusiasm began at the end of 1962, after an interval of at least 10 years. I had never seen a ten-coupled locomotive but did not have long to wait. In those first few weeks, during a snatched 10min beside the Midland main line to the north of St Albans, in the gloom of a late winter's afternoon, No 92021, one of the Crewe-built engines, was photographed on a main line freight. I was at the time unaware that, of the 251 built, my first sighting was one of the 10 Crosti-boilered engines. For years a Cricklewood engine, her movement, as with many of the class, became erratic in the final few years. No 92021 ended her days at Birkenhead, a fact unknown to me until coming to write these words. Perhaps I may end this chapter by listing my '9F' photographs: this indicates not only my movements but also the geographical spread of these most successful locomotives. My listing is done in chronological order, and for the detailed information my thanks are due to Peter Hands and his series of invaluable reference books, *What Happened to Steam?*

Number	Photographed	Location	ShedCode/Home Depot		Withdrawn
92021*	11.62	North of St Albans	15A	Cricklewood	11.67
92145	3.63	King's Cross: Top Shed	34E	Peterborough:	2.66
92184	3.63	King's Cross: Top Shed	34E	New England	2.65
92128	8.63	Near Radlett	21A	Saltley	11.67
92001	25.9.63	Winchfield	2A	Tyseley	1.67
92042	4.2.64	March	40E	Colwick	12.65
92174	4.2.64	March	36A	Doncaster	12.65
92025*	4.2.64	March	15B	Wellingborough	11.67
92022*	1.4.64	Peak Forest	16J	Rowsley	11.67
92083	6.6.64	Blackwell	15C	Kettering	2.67
92230	6.6.64	Lickey	85D	Bromsgrove	12.65
92123	3.10.64	Feltham	15A	Leicester (Midland)	10.67
92159	3.12.64	Newton Heath	9D	Newton Heath	7.67
92024*	4.7.65	Birkenhead	8H	Birkenhead	11.67
92069	11.7.65	Edge Hill	8H	Birkenhead	5.68
92092	11.7.65	Edge Hill	8H	Birkenhead	10.66
92157	11.7.65	Birkenhead	8H	Birkenhead	9.67
92011	8.8.65	Birkenhead	8H	Birkenhead	11.67
92086	8.8.65	Birkenhead	8H	Birkenhead	11.67
92102	3.10.65	Birkenhead	8H	Birkenhead	11.67
92123	3.10.65	Birkenhead	8H	Birkenhead	10.67
92166	3.10.65	Birkenhead	8H	Birkenhead	11.67
92047	30.10.65	Bidston	8H	Birkenhead	9.67
92079	9.1.66	Birkenhead	8H	Birkenhead	11.67
92165	7.5.66	Birkenhead	8H	Birkenhead	3.68
92204	18.7.66	Stourbridge	2A	Tyseley	12.67
92030	9.9.66	Derby	2D	Banbury	2.67
92132	9.3.67	Stoke-on-Trent	8B	Warrington	10.67
92054	10.8.67	Speke Junction	8C	Speke Junction	5.68
92223	25.6.68	Carnforth	10A	Carnforth	4.68
92249	26.6.68	Speke Junction	8C	Speke Junction	5.68
92094	26.6.68	Speke Junction	8C	Speke Junction	5.68

*Crosti-boilered locomotives.

Perhaps it is my dedication to numbers that fascinates me about this numerical detail and information. Perhaps the most obvious comment to make is that, unlike the WD 2-10-0s, the '9Fs' were widely distributed around Britain, with the exception of the Scottish Region: it is probable, therefore, that Carlisle Kingmoor was the only motive power depot in Britain that ever had two types of ten-coupled locomotive allocated: another nugget of information that I do not recall having read elsewhere. How strange it is that, almost 20 years after steam's elimination from British Rail, the detail about thousands of individual locomotives which is now available enables me — and presumably numerous other enthusiasts — to subject one's lists of numbers noted and photographs taken, to scrutiny, and to search for coincidence, repetition, distant sightings and other interesting items of information. With this in mind, let me test your tolerance somewhat by extrapolating my list from one in chronological to numerical order. I have divided them into batches, in accordance with the batches in which they were ordered and built. We now have my sightings set out in the accompanying table — excluding obviously the unidentified members of the class photographed at Birkenhead; on the Lickey; and at Mold Junction on 20 March 1966.

Joy of joys! At least all the work implicit in compiling these lists has brought its own reward — and an extraordinary coincidence. Not until doing this 'research' have I discovered that my camera captured '9F' No 92123 at Feltham — an unlikely occurrence in itself — on 3 October 1964, and again on shed at Birkenhead precisely a year to the day later. Naturally my photography was geographically related to my own movements, disciplined as they were by commitments to family life in Berkshire, Somerset and Sussex; Parliamentary candidature in Birkenhead and Bristol; and my reasonably roving commercial movements, which I tended to direct, as far as possible, to steam areas.

Lest this chapter becomes an eternal soliloquy it must close with a reminder yet again of the rarity, in the one and a half centuries of British locomotive construction, of the ten-coupled machine; and the dominant role played, at the 12th hour, of those fine, Riddles engines. This is not in any sense a technical book; rather is it a personal record of locomotives of

Number	Built
92001 (a)	Crewe 1954
92011	Crewe 1954
92021 (b)	Crewe 1955
92022 (b)	Crewe 1955
92024 (b)	Crewe 1955
92025 (b)	Crewe 1955
92030	Crewe 1954/5
92042	Crewe 1954/5
92047	Crewe 1954/5
92054	Crewe 1955/6
92069	Crewe 1955/6
92079 (a) (c)	Crewe 1955/6
92083	Crewe 1955/6
92086	Crewe 1955/6
92092	Swindon 1956/7
92094	Swindon 1956/7
92102	Crewe 1956/7
92123	Crewe 1956/7
92128	Crewe 1956/7
92132	Crewe 1956/7
92145	Crewe 1957/8
92157	Crewe 1957/8
92159	Crewe 1957/8
92165 (d)	Crewe 1957/8
92166 (d)	Crewe 1957/8
92174	Crewe 1957/8
92184 (e)	Swindon 1957/8
92204 (e)	Swindon 1959/60
92223 (e)	Crewe 1958
92230 (e)	Crewe 1958
92249	Crewe 1958

Notes
(a) Subsequently fitted with double blastpipe and chimney.
(b) Crosti-boiler engines, converted later to conventional exhaust system: not then fitted with smoke deflectors and retaining smaller boiler and firebox.
(c) Former Lickey Banker.
(d) Equipped with Berkley Mechanical Stoker: removed in 1962.
(e) Built with double blastpipe and chimney.

Left:
'Big Bertha' in all her glory. Pregnant with latent power, No 2290 was 'unique' — that most ill-used word. Seen here at Bromsgrove in 1921 after the fitting of electric light to the smokebox door, and converted for oil-burning due to coal strike. She was renumbered 22290 by the LMS in 1947, 58100 by British Railways, and withdrawn in 1956. What a candidate she should have been for preservation.

which I am aware but never saw, and of those that I was fortunate enough to photograph. Not even in this chapter have I sought remotely to catalogue anything other than superficial detail. Tenders, although important, failed to engender much interest at the time of my photography. Numerous learned tomes set out detailed information on this and other important subjects, and there is no better series than that by Brian Haresnape, whose pictorial record and written word complement each other superbly.

4-6-0

Whilst the world's first 4-6-0 was built in the United States and *not* at Swindon, it was surely in this country that the type was perfected and where it achieved pre-eminence. Everything is bigger (but by no means better) in North America, so they were building six- and eight-coupled locomotives at an early date, and of course went on to construct monsters the like of which our railways never needed. In retrospect, nevertheless, it seems surprising that 47 years elapsed between 1847, when that transatlantic machine appeared, designed for heavy, plodding freight work in a mountainous region, and the arrival on the scene, in 1894, of David Jones' 'Big Goods' on the Highland Railway, the nearest region in Britain remotely to resemble the terrain which dictated the earlier requirement in the United States.

Two years after the 'Jones Goods' created British history, it was indeed Swindon that turned out the first English 4-6-0, when No 36 emerged as the brain-child of William Dean. Although experimental, No 36 was by no means revolutionary, with its inside cylinders and outside frames very much bearing the Dean hallmark. This engine too was intended for use on the heavy South Wales freight and mineral traffic. Although the next Swindon 4-6-0, No 2601, led on to a class of 2-6-0s (see Chapter 8), it bore the influence and stamp, with its domeless boiler, of the man who, more than any other, laid the foundation for that pre-eminence of the 4-6-0 in Britain — George Jackson Churchward. We shall return to him shortly.

Whilst the first two 4-6-0s were intended purely as goods engines, David Jones' machine undertook plenty of passenger traffic during the holiday season, and it was only his untimely early retirement that precluded his claiming the distinction of designing and introducing the first passenger engine of this wheel-arrangement. Indeed, his successor, Peter Drummond, modified the 'Jones Passenger' and the

resultant 'Castle' class entered the scene in 1900, just a year behind Britain's first passenger 4-6-0 — that designed by William Worsdell for the North Eastern Railway.

Already in this chapter, the name of 'Churchward' and the class of 'Castle' have been used, albeit not connected. The story of the 4-6-0 has a long way to go before Churchward's successor introduced the 'Castle' class on the Great Western — arguably one of the best locomotives ever to run on any railway, anywhere. At the turn of the century the 4-2-2 was still almost universally acknowledged as acceptable motive power for fast main line work. Indeed, as late as 1906, the GWR had 80 4-2-2s, and only 18 4-6-0s, and it was not until 1909 that the number of the latter exceeded that of the former. However, Churchward was by now well in the saddle at Swindon, and he was to chart the future for Great Western motive power based firmly on the 4-6-0. From 'Saints',

Top right:
The masterpiece of British locomotive design — Great Western Railway 'Castle' class 4-6-0 No 7018 *Drysllwyn Castle* awaits her next turn of duty on Old Oak Common MPD in March 1963. One of the final manifestations of the class originally introduced in 1923, No 7018 was not built until May 1949 in BR days, and the double chimney somewhat disfigured what otherwise was the most elegant of locomotives. The elbow steam pipes were a distinctive feature of 'Kings' and 'Castles'. By the standards of the 'Castle' class, No 7018 was shortlived, being withdrawn in September 1963.

Right:
Perutz film produced great clarity of detail, as evidenced by this shot of a clean Stanier 'Black Five' 4-6-0 No 45270 at Camden on 28 April 1963. The 842 engines of this class were not only the most numerous but perhaps the most reliable mixed-traffic engines ever built in Britain. No 45270 was withdrawn in July 1967 from Crewe South Shed and scrapped at Cashmores, Great Bridge, in January 1968.

'Ladies' and 'Counts'; and his 'Stars', 'Knights', 'Kings', 'Queens', 'Princes', 'Princesses' and 'Abbeys', were to flow the 'Castles', 'Kings', 'Halls', 'Granges', 'Manors' and 'Counties' of Collett and Hawksworth.

It is no part of my purpose to seek to write even a simple potted history of the wheel-arrangements and types of locomotive chosen. That task has been carried out by a number of learned and eminent authors of railway books. All I can do is to try to communicate the impact of the various types on the railway scene as I saw and recorded it in those final years. Nevertheless, one can dream, surely, of the unattainable proposition of colour film to record those vivid liveries in the Pre-Grouping years. Imagine the sight of those Manson 4-6-0s on the Glasgow & South Western, or Robinson's Great Central engines on the Grimsby fish-trains; and 400 ASA would have been manna from heaven with which to record *Cardean*, undoubtedly the most famous of the Caledonian 4-6-0s.

Enough of these fantasies! To return to my real world, I can readily recall my excitement at what

transpired to be my first photograph of a Pre-Grouping 4-6-0. It was a grey, gloomy February day in 1963. My wife Jane having 'decided' on an outdoor hobby for me, and I having selected railway photography as the appropriate occupation, the Saturday mornings in those first few weeks became my time of initiation. We were both working, so she needed time for shopping, whilst I was encouraged to 'tramp the tracks'. I had barely looked at a steam engine or read any railway literature between leaving school in 1952, and taking the first colour photograph of my 'photographic career' in November 1962.

With the intensity of interest nowadays in the steam era, and having devoted myself to the subject *since* the end of 1962, it is perhaps hard to explain how ignorant I had become about railway matters, not in any case that I had ever been more than an average 'spotter' whose time was spent at the platform end. From my first re-encounter with steam in November 1962, I had in fact to educate myself virtually from scratch. My records indicate, and my memory confirms, brief visits to King's Cross, Kensington Olympia, Luton Midland Road and St Pancras stations in November 1962; so far my hesitant first steps took me again no further than a station platform end. The following month, during a visit to Jane's parents in Burnham-on-Sea, I ventured to Highbridge S&D station, and crept hesitantly off the platform end, to gain the tiny shed and servicing area. Nobody apprehended me, and I became emboldened.

At the turn of the year I 'escaped' again from 'In-laws Duty' and this time made off for the day from Burnham to Bristol. What riches awaited me there! On that day, 26 January 1963, my cup

Below:
'The Crocodile' No 36 was the first English 4-6-0, emerging with the Dean *imprimatur*, from Swindon in August 1896. Two years behind the 'Jones Goods' on the Highland, this odd engine, unlike its Scottish predecessors, was singularly problematical. It carried the only large boiler ever built entirely to Dean's ideas. Although allocated to Newport for working heavy freights through the Severn tunnel, it seems to have spent an inordinate amount of its short life at Swindon Works, prior to withdrawal in December 1905.

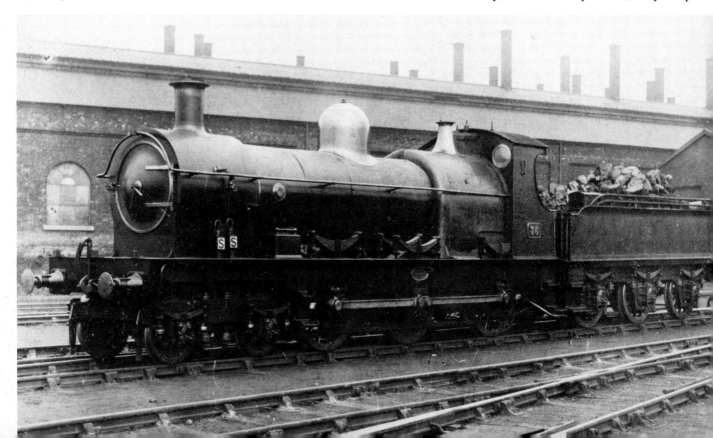

Above:
Six years after the 'Jones Goods' had earned its place in history, the 'Castle' class 4-6-0 emerged on the Highland Railway. Although attributed to Peter Drummond, the HR 'Castles' were the passenger engine derivative of David Jones 'Goods' of 1894. These fine engines enjoyed both long lives and enviable reputations, and merit their place in any chapter on the British 4-6-0. Here, No 140 *Taymouth Castle* stands at Perth, with a well-filled tender.

overflowed with GWR, LMS and BR joy. Indeed, entry 'A1' in my catalogue of photographs, which is not totally chronological, is BR Standard Class 5MT 4-6-0 No 73031, standing at the head of the much-delayed 10.40 Bristol to Newcastle through train, under the awning of Brunel's Train Shed. Never did I dream of seeing that photograph reproduced in a book — let alone a book comprising my own photographs and words. (It can be seen in *Call of Steam*.) What is more, my wildest imagination did not include becoming an MP in Bristol seven years later, and then some years after that playing a small part in saving and restoring the Train Shed, as a trustee of the Brunel Engineering Centre Trust. I ramble on and digress. . .

The other 4-6-0s, seen and photographed that day, included Standard Class 5 No 73094, GWR 'Hall' No 6927 *Lilford Hall*, 'County' No 1009 *County of Carmarthen*, LMS 'Black 5' No 45269 — indeed it seems an interesting enough bunch of locomotives to warrant listing, together with their home sheds, at the time my photographs at Bristol were taken that January day. There were seven different classes of the same wheel-arrangement on that one day, and doubtless there were more which I may have seen but did not photograph due either to the need to harbour scarce resources in the cost of colour film, or to unphotogenic positions. Anyway, for an early foray in my 'career', this seems a good 'bag' in retrospect.

4-6-0s photographed at Bristol 26 January 1963:

County

1009	*County of Carmarthen*	(82B Taunton)

Hall

4951	*Pendeford Hall*	(81F Oxford — transferred to 82C Swindon the following month)
4955	*Plaspower Hall*	(83B Taunton — transferred to 86G Pontypool Road, the following month)
4998	*Eyton Hall*	(84C Banbury)
6925	*Hackness Hall*	(84B Oxley)
6927	*Lilford Hall*	(81F Oxford)

Castle

5038	*Morlais Castle*	(81D Reading)
7022	*Hereford Castle*	(83D Plymouth Laira)

Grange

6800	*Arlington Grange*	(86G Pontypool Road)

Modified Hall

6980	*Llanrumney Hall*	(84B Oxley)

Manor

7815	*Fritwell Manor*	(87G Carmarthen)

Stanier 'Black Five'

45269		(21A Saltley)

Jubilee

4562 ?		Unidentified

BR Standard Class 5

73015		(82E Bristol Barrow Road)
73031		(85C Gloucester Barnwood)
73094		(85C Gloucester Barnwood)

This is the first occasion on which I have carried out this exercise, of listing all the locomotives — let alone as specialised a task as listing all the locomotives of a single wheel-arrangement — that I managed to photograph at a given place on a given date. It proves to be most interesting. Firstly, only one of these engines appears to be Bristol-based. Secondly, they illustrate the versatility of the 4-6-0 by enabling one, through contemplation, to work out the wide variety of duties — passenger, parcels, freight — that these locomotives must have worked or were about to work. Thirdly, they emphasise the key inter-regional role of Bristol: and fourthly, by checking the information obtained through the estimable Peter Hands' *What Happened to Steam* series, they remind us of the fate befallen by those former GWR steam locomotives which found themselves at sheds like Oxlcy that were transferred out of Western Region control.

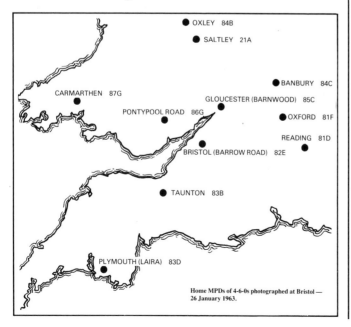

OXLEY 84B
SALTLEY 21A
BANBURY 84C
CARMARTHEN 87G
GLOUCESTER (BARNWOOD) 85C
PONTYPOOL ROAD 86G
OXFORD 81F
READING 81D
BRISTOL (BARROW ROAD) 82E
TAUNTON 83B
PLYMOUTH (LAIRA) 83D

Home MPDs of 4-6-0s photographed at Bristol — 26 January 1963.

The following month, February 1963, saw me emerging from the warmth of our Chiswick flat on a Saturday morning, in search of steam in London. It was a predictably grey and gloomy day when I gained the island platform at Battersea's Queenstown Road station. Still in my very formative first few photographic forays, my knowledge was scant, my information similar. Were there 'Lord Nelsons' and 'King Arthurs' to be seen? My childhood experiences as a Southern 'spotter' were virtually all there was on which to base my expectations, and they were restricted to the south coast. To the romantic visions of 'Nelsons' and 'Arthurs' was vaguely grafted in my mind the existence of less-glamorous 4-6-0s of uncertain vintage. As I peered through the murk of that February morning, awaiting events, my choice as to which end of the platform on which to stand was influenced by the tantalising sight of distant, rising steam and smoke in the Waterloo direction, or the compositional advantage of the girder bridge the other way. I took up position initially at the south-western end of the island platform, almost underneath that girder bridge, which carries the former LBSCR and SECR lines from Victoria over

Above:
GWR No 7824 *Iford Manor* pounds the beat on the SECR Reading-Redhill line, in charge of the 10.42 Wolverhampton-Ramsgate train, twixt Gomshall & Shere and Dorking, on 20 July 1963. Of the 30 'Manors' introduced in 1938, no less than nine have survived. 7824 was not one of the lucky ones. Presumably, being an Oxley (84B) engine she had worked this train through from Wolverhampton, although an Oxford engine change was customary on many NW/SE through trains. Of light weight for a 4-6-0, 'Manors' were regular performers on the SECR route.

Below:
Breasting the top of the Lickey Incline with a lengthy freight, and with banking assistance from a '9F' 2-10-0 out of sight 'down the hill', comes LMS 'Black Five' No 45310, on a 'summer' day: it is 6 June 1964. This was an unforgettable day, not only for the insistent downpour, but also for my first and last visit to the 'Lickey Inclined Plane' (see page 26) for steam action.

the LSWR lines alongside which my vigil commenced. Only the colour light signals pierced the gloom and all-pervading greyness of lighting conditions that would have daunted and deterred any serious photographer.

First to appear out of the gloom was a BR Standard Class 3MT 2-6-2T on empty stock duty, before the inevitable stream of Bulleid Pacifics in both directions. At this date the Southern Region still controlled the former LSWR lines west of Salisbury, so even on a winter Saturday there were trains to destinations that have long since been eradicated from the railway network. Notwithstanding the appearance, light engine, of BR Standard Class 5MT 4-6-0 No 73119 *Elaine*, bearing the name of an erstwhile 'King Arthur' class, my hopes of seeing a prewar, let alone Pre-Grouping locomotive, seemed unlikely to be fulfilled. Bear in mind that I had no detailed knowledge of BR steam stock, the pace of withdrawal and scrapping, or indeed more than a passing acquaintance with or awareness of the works of Drummond or of Urie, and you may understand my excitement when, galloping under the girder bridge, came a 4-6-0 clearly of mature years. It was travelling light engine pretty fast on the up slow line, namely the most northerly track at this busy point. As at this time I was blissfully unaware of local railway geography, it did not occur to me that it was probably heading for Nine Elms Shed, the location of which I was quite ignorant. Indeed not for some time did I realise that that rising smoke and steam visible in the distance towards Waterloo, emanated from engines leaving the shed and awaiting a path to run down to the terminus. If my 4-6-0 was indeed heading for Nine Elms it would have had to cross every track to gain the shed — a formidable movement for the signalman to plot if

delays to up and down trains, most of which were electrics, were to be avoided. However, I reminisce and digress from the locomotive in question — its number was 30515. It was with real excitement that I thumbed feverishly through my Ian Allan *Locomotives and Locoshed Book*.

The first 4-6-0 to be built by the London and South Western Railway emerged from the cross-fertilisation of men, their ideas, and the machines they built, that existed between the LSWR and its Scottish contemporaries. The interplay of personalities between Nine Elms and St Rollox, illustrated by Dugald Drummond's visit to J. F. McIntosh, resulted in the first LSWR 4-6-0s, of which little is now written, probably due to their mediocrity. These '330' class engines, however, were the forerunners of Dugald Drummond's later efforts, culminating in his Class T14 'Paddlebox'. The link between LSWR and Scotland was, sadly, related not only to design. Drummond, like David Jones on the Highland, suffered a serious footplate accident, following which the amputation of a leg caused his death from shock the following day. Drummond was succeeded as Chief Mechanical Engineer of the LSWR by his Works Manager, Robert Urie, who himself had been Chief Draughtsman of the Caledonian at the beginning of the McIntosh era, and subsequently Works Manager at St Rollox.

To claim any similarity between the 'Jones Goods' and Urie's first 4-6-0, which emerged in 1913, would be somewhat spurious, save only to be able to claim that the concept of this wheel-arrangement in Britain does seem to have been fostered by our northern citizens. Indeed, Urie's 'H15s' bore little direct relationship even to his predecessor's design; but the Scots' affinity to the 4-6-0 manifested itself, in the 'H15', in what O. S. Nock has described as 'in its

layout of the machinery, the true prototype of the British steam locomotive in its most critical and final age'.

To pretend that any of this historic tracery was prompted by the sight of Urie 'S15' No 30515 scurrying through Queenstown Road Battersea station on that February morning in 1963, would be to attempt to deceive.

The Urie 'H15' 4-6-0, although designated a mixed-traffic locomotive, was successfully used on some of the main LSWR express passenger trains.

Above:
Experimental rebuild of LNWR 'Experiment' class 4-6-0 No 1361, latterly LMS No 5554 *Prospero*, seen here passing Dudley Port. George Whale's 'Experiment' class had 6ft 3in driving wheels in place of the 6ft 9in wheels on his 'Precursor' class. *Prospero* was rebuilt with four cylinders arranged on the Dendy Marshall system and with a superheater. The Whale 4-4-0 'Precursors', and the 4-6-0 'Experiments' and '19in Goods' epitomised the 'Crewe Look'.

Below:
Francis William Webb's prototype 'Bill Bailey' 4-6-0, of the London & North Western Railway. Unfussy, but not stark; neat but not fancy; surely the epitome of a locomotive built to work, and built to last — albeit not eventually a LNWR 'classic' class, and consigned almost to oblivion by the passage of time.

Above:
By 1965, any 4-6-0 remaining at work on Southern Region, other than the Standard classes, was a welcome sight. Maunsell 'S15' No 30833 was no exception; from the 1927 batch, she was one of only three to survive into that year. Here at Feltham, her home shed, on 23 January 1965, she had but a few weeks' life left. These engines handled fast freights on the former LSWR main lines competently and well for many years, and with their Urie predecessors, were amongst my favourite engines.

Below:
Amongst my small number of LNER locomotive photographs there is, unsurprisingly, a preponderance of 'B1s'. As assessed by history, they always lived somewhat in the shadow of their LMS counterpart the 'Black Fives'. Weak sunshine casts light on the wheels, rust and grime of No 61207, at home on Peterborough New England shed on 7 July 1963, some five months before withdrawal. This, I am afraid, is how my generation recalls those final years of BR steam.

For that railway the modern 4-6-0 had been born. Urie followed up with a true express passenger engine, the 'N15', which in turn was the undoubted forerunner of Maunsell's 'King Arthurs'. As the 'N15' was to the 'Arthurs', so the Urie 'S15' was to the Maunsell version of the same class. That is why I have spent the last few paragraphs relating back to No 30515. Perhaps in that first photograph of a Pre-Grouping 4-6-0 was born an unrealised awareness of the significance of what I saw. That may seem unlikely pompous nonsense, but it certainly was the birth of an affection for Urie's 'S15' that has stood the test of time. They remain one of my firm favourites.

Seeking a link between one chosen class and another, for purely anecdotal purposes, is not too hard. From the Urie 'S15' to the GWR 'Castle' 4-6-0 may seem an odd juxtaposition. The name James Clayton gives me my excuse to change the subject. In 1919 he was promoted to be Personal Assistant to the Chief Mechanical Engineer of the South Eastern and Chatham Railway and in that role was in regular contact with his counterparts in the other railway companies prior to and after the 1923 Grouping, at which time he became Personal Assistant to Richard Maunsell. Clayton was a fervent admirer of Churchward, with whom he had just come into contact after his 1919 promotion. Thus when Maunsell and the SR turned their attention to future front-line locomotives, and the 'Pacific-or-4-6-0' question arose, Clayton used his admiration for things Great Western to influence the decision. His

66

Facing page, top:
If railway enthusiasts were to search for a guiding light to portend the future, that search could well end with the *Polar Star* — the class, if not this specific member thereof. Where Churchward led the rest would follow. His classic lines, here portrayed by 'Star' class 4-6-0 No 4005, built at Swindon Works in March 1907, need little further amplification — which is just as well, because neither date nor location is recorded in this fine study from the Library of the National Railway Museum. No 4005 was withdrawn in November 1934.

Facing page, bottom:
On page 18 is shown a Drummond 'T14' in original glory and condition. In postwar Southern green, sister engine No 443, rebuilt by Maunsell in 1931, rests on Nine Elms Shed in 1945. No longer is the 'Paddlebox' nickname appropriate since removal of the cumbersome but distinctive 'Paddlebox' splasher which caused overheating of the axleboxes; the stovepipe chimney seems sadly in keeping with her run-down appearance. She was withdrawn in May 1949 without receiving a BR number.

Left:
In her declining years, but still with style, Urie LSWR 'H15' 2-cylinder 4-6-0 No 482 has charge of a down goods at Hook in 1946. These engines were the forerunners of the classic Maunsell Southern Railway 4-6-0s.

Below:
Unmistakably Churchward, unmistakably Great Western; 'Star' class 4-6-0 No 4049 *Princess Maud* speeds an up Worcester express at Ruscombe, in 1939. The continuity from 'Saints' and 'Stars', to 'Halls' and 'Castles', 'Kings' and 'Counties', is taken for granted by enthusiasts and historians, but is surely unparalleled worldwide on any railway, or any mode of transport, by land, sea or air — or am I biased?

Above:
The longer outside steampipe and the plate frame on the front of the leading bogie identify this as a Hawksworth 'Modified Hall' from a class introduced in 1944. Some of the 71 engines were built after nationalisation and when added to the 258 'Halls' introduced in 1924, caused a headache to those responsible for finding suitable names of Halls on GWR territory, a task ultimately quietly abandoned, when out-of-area names had to be given. Here, at Reading MPD on 7 November 1964, No 6991 *Acton Burnell Hall* has already lost her nameplate, but not her style, which is unmistakably Great Western. The 81D shedplate indicates she is at her home shed, to which she was allocated in April 1963; a month after this photograph was taken she was transferred to 81E Didcot; the following July to 81F Oxford from which shed she was withdrawn at the end of Western steam in December 1965.

Below:
Stanier three-cylinder 'Jubilee' 4-6-0 No 45647 *Sturdee* runs off the LNWR main line into Patricroft MPD on 5 March 1965. The scene is redolent with the atmosphere of the steam railway; semaphore signals, ample junctions, huts, bridges — and the tall chimneys of Patricroft station in the distance, to the left of the base of 45647's tender. The line running parallel to and behind the locomotive originally ran northeast up to join the L&Y at Molyneux Junction, near Clifton Junction. Patricroft, with its shed in the triangle of lines, the third arm of which ran northwest off the main line, to Bolton, was an excellent 'pitch' at the end of steam. Those 6ft 9in 'Jubilee' wheels somehow epitomised Stanier's transformation of LMS motive power; large wheels still, but modern taper boiler development of the 'Patriot' class. Although, at the date of this photograph, allocated to Farnley Junction, *Sturdee* was one of the Leeds Holbeck (55A) engines to form the final active cluster of these elegant locomotives, surviving until April 1967.

verdict was confirmed after footplate rides on a 'Castle' non-stop from Paddington to Plymouth, followed by a journey, 10 days later, on the footplate of a Gresley Pacific from King's Cross to Grantham.

Obviously the Bulleid Pacifics destroy the proposition that GWR and SR were 4-6-0 railways, whilst the LMS and LNER favoured the 4-6-2. However, the Bulleid locomotives were really an 'out-of-time' exception to the story of the (Post-Grouping) developments of the 'Big Four', whilst the 'Arthurs' and 'Nelsons' were the top link SR locomotives and, as already mentioned, the 'S15s' were the freight version of the 'Arthurs'. By the end of 1962 when my photography commenced, the Urie 'S15' was the only Pre-Grouping 4-6-0 of Southern Railway heritage still at work. On the Western Region, naturally, the 4-6-0 still held sway — insofar as steam could be 'holding sway' anywhere on BR by this twilight hour, notwithstanding the withdrawal of the 'Kings' at the end of 1962.

It is no part of my intention to undervalue the obvious and vital role of the 4-6-0 as a top link passenger locomotive. The 'Royal Scot', 'Patriot' and 'Jubilee' classes on the LMS are well-enough documented, and even as late as November 1962 I was able to photograph 'Jubilee' No 45569 *Tasmania* pulling out of St Pancras at the head of the Saturdays-only 11.50 train to Bradford Forster Square. Indeed, the rebuilt 'Royal Scot' is a formidable rival to the 'Castle', 'King' or 'Nelson's' claim to the title 'Britain's Most Powerful 4-6-0'. Sadly, I was able only to see a handful of the dwindling band of these fine locomotives, including No 46141 *The North Staffordshire Regiment* and

Below:

Writing captions for photographs one has not taken is not only a new but also a somewhat unsatisfactory experience, as one is obliged to make vague generalisations. The 'Claughton' 4-6-0s of the LNWR clearly merit mention and attention in this chapter. Contemporary historians used adjectives as diverse as 'magnificent' to 'disappointing', Fowler used the experience to create the 'Patriots', some of which Stanier rebuilt; but certain it is that they did not encourage Stanier to derive or develop therefrom. Built at Crewe in 1917, LNWR No 1085 became LMS No 5954, withdrawal taking place in December 1932. Such a short life rarely befell Great Western 4-6-0s of this vintage. Visible amongst detail alterations made to some of the 'Claughtons' towards the end of the LNWR's existence and which can be seen here are the lamp irons, cut-away buffer beam corners, large reversing-gear cover, and two oil boxes on the handrail.

Right:

If Webb's 'Bill Bailey' class is not accorded a place in popular railway history, then the 'Jones Goods' most certainly is. Britain's first 4-6-0 was withdrawn for preservation in 1935, but the class continued in service for some years. A member of the class stands outside the diminutive shed at Dingwall, in 1939.

Below right:

Whilst some 4-6-0s gained immortality, others rarely emerged into the limelight, had short lives and were consigned to oblivion. Some, however, generate a spark of interest and Webb's LNWR 4-cylinder compound mixed traffic engines of 1903 vintage were one such class. Known as 'Bill Baileys' they were Webb's last design. Although continued by Whale after his succession, they gained a dubious reputation as troublesome. Here is No 2033, built at Crewe in June 1903 and seen in the works yard. She was withdrawn in April 1914.

Above:

Summer rain has put a glisten on the clean paintwork of BR Standard '4' 4-6-0 No 75077, at this date a Basingstoke engine, as she canters, light engine, down the fast line between Fleet and Winchfield, on the LSWR main line, on 25 June 1965. Such mundane artefacts as lineside telegraph poles, with that bewitching rise and fall of the wires, are now a rarity, whilst the first few accoutrements of third-rail electrification, visible here, are today part of a changed scene where no steam has run since July 1967. No 75077 lasted until the end of Southern steam, being withdrawn in July 1967.

Right:

The setting winter sun glints on the smokebox door of Kingmoor 'Black Five' No 44726, on shed at Patricroft on 1 December 1964. Although this was the most numerous class of British 4-6-0, variants were comparatively few. This however, is one of 10 members of the class fitted with a steel firebox and 44726 seems also to have acquired a snow plough, albeit barely big enough to cope with the blizzards that had marked the winter two years previously. Note the water tower on the right of the picture.

No 46115 *Scots Guardsman* at Willesden in March 1963. I never saw — or at least not through my lens, and not that I remember — the 'Scots' as they were in their LMS heyday, as immortalised in the photographs of Eric Treacy at Edge Hill, Liverpool. Likewise, the 'Patriot' class, my record of which is naturally restricted to a handful of the rebuilt engines, including No 45530 *Sir Frank Ree* that March day 1963, at Willesden. The Urie 'S15' to me was, to its Maunsell successor, as attractive as the 'Scots' and 'Patriots' in comparison to their rebuilt successors. Somehow those LMS rebuilds looked 'Stanier-Standard' but that is certainly not intended to be one iota derogatory or rude.

To mention Stanier in the context of the 4-6-0 is to think automatically of probably the most reliable and versatile steam locomotive ever built. The 'Black Five' was and is the very epitome of the title of this

'Lord Nelson' class 4-6-0 No 30855 *Robert Blake* waits at signals at Southampton Central in 1957. On their introduction in 1926 the Southern Railway proclaimed these engines the 'most powerful 4-6-0 in Britain'. Probably just out-shopped from Eastleigh, No 30855 was withdrawn in September 1961.

chapter. It was a far cry indeed from the early 4-6-0s of the English constituent companies of the LMS, of which F. W. Webb's '1400' or 'Bill Bailey' class comes to mind. Although the first of these long, long-departed engines did not emerge from Crewe Works until February 1903, it looked every inch a Victorian locomotive — not least because of the Webb wheels, with their small number of spokes. Notwithstanding the fact that Webb's successor George Whale built a few more, the 'Bill Baileys' were scrapped steadily from 1913 onwards. The passenger aspect of their 'mixed traffic' designation never proved satisfactory. To my amateur eye, the wheels on the Whale engines *looked* a little different, although obviously they were the same size. No documentation, however, seems to bear out my visual opinion.

If the 'Bill Baileys' were a failure, then Whale's own inside-cylinder 4-6-0s were not: 420 of these LNWR standard locomotives were built between 1905 and 1922 as between the 'Experiment', '19in Goods' and the 'Prince of Wales', Bowen-Cooke's superheated version of the 'Experiments'. It is not just bias that requires me to state that the LNWR's

four-cylinder 4-6-0s never really reached the performance levels of Churchward's locomotives on the GWR. However, in 1913 Bowen-Cooke produced his own design of 4-6-0. These engines, the 'Claughtons', reputedly put up some outstanding individual performances, but again overall were not up to the all-round quality, economy and reliability of the GWR 'Stars' or 'Saints'. Of the other LMS constituent companies, the Lancashire & Yorkshire sired the Hughes 4-6-0 in 1908. In 1920 one was rebuilt with superheater and piston valves, dramatically improved and then destined, along with the LNWR 'Claughtons', to play their part in the LMS 4-6-0 saga, which blossomed only with the arrival of William Stanier from Swindon.

This is not a history book, let alone any attempt seriously to appraise the role of classes or types of locomotives. All I am doing is to trace the arrival on the scene of such 4-6-0s as I was able to see and photograph between 1962 and 1968. In a nutshell, one might summarise the position thus:

GWR — continuity Pre- to Post-Grouping, Churchward to Collett to Hawksworth

SR — direct link from Urie to Maunsell

LMS — progression from Whale to Bowen-Cooke (LNWR) and from Hughes (L&Y) (as well as Highland and Caledonian) to Stanier

LNER — no natural follow through from Pre-

Grouping Great Eastern, North Eastern or Great Central engines, by Gresley.

The LNER was not, of course, bereft of 4-6-0s. But Gresley's 'B17' was the response to a specific motive-power requirement on former Great Eastern territory, rather than a manifestation by the railway's CME of his belief, *per se*, in the universal application of this wheel-arrangement throughout his territory. It was left to Gresley's successor Edward Thompson to produce the only locomotive of this wheel-arrangement built in sufficient numbers to qualify as a major contributor in its own right to a role in the story of the British 4-6-0.

Introduced in 1942, the 'B1' 4-6-0s, Thompson's most successful and least problematical class, eventually numbered 410 locomotives; although in fact No 61057 was scrapped in 1950 following a collision at Chelmsford, at about the time that the last of the class emerged from the manufacturers. Forty locomotives of the original series were named after members of the South African antelope species. These two-cylinder engines eventually replaced hordes of varied GNR, GCR and NER Atlantics, various GCR 4-6-0s and 4-4-0s from all the LNER constituent companies. As with the '8Fs' and 'Black Fives' from the LMS they were the last class of the LNER to represent 'their' railway in any numbers.

The early Grouping years, in the 1920s, really saw the 4-6-0 at its zenith as challenger for the role of leading British express passenger locomotive type.

The success of the GWR 'Castles' on LMS and LNER metals seemed, in 1927, to indicate that, although obviously smaller than the rival Pacifics, they would outperform their bigger brothers. The fact that, ultimately, a good 'big 'un' can outdo a good 'little 'un', does not one whit detract from the vital role that the British 4-6-0 played in our nation's steam story. My reference earlier to the rebuilt 'Scots', 'Patriots' and 'Jubilees' as well as the 'Kings' and 'Castles', 'Arthurs' and 'Nelsons', illustrates that, at their best, they were more than 'just mixed traffic machines' albeit outshone on Top Link duties by 'Coronations', 'A4s' and latterly Bulleid Pacifics.

Notwithstanding my predilection for the 'S15', or my admiration for the GWR 4-6-0s, it is surely Stanier's 'Black Five' that earns the accolade for ultimate versatility, reliability and indeed longevity within this truncated history of the British 4-6-0. The

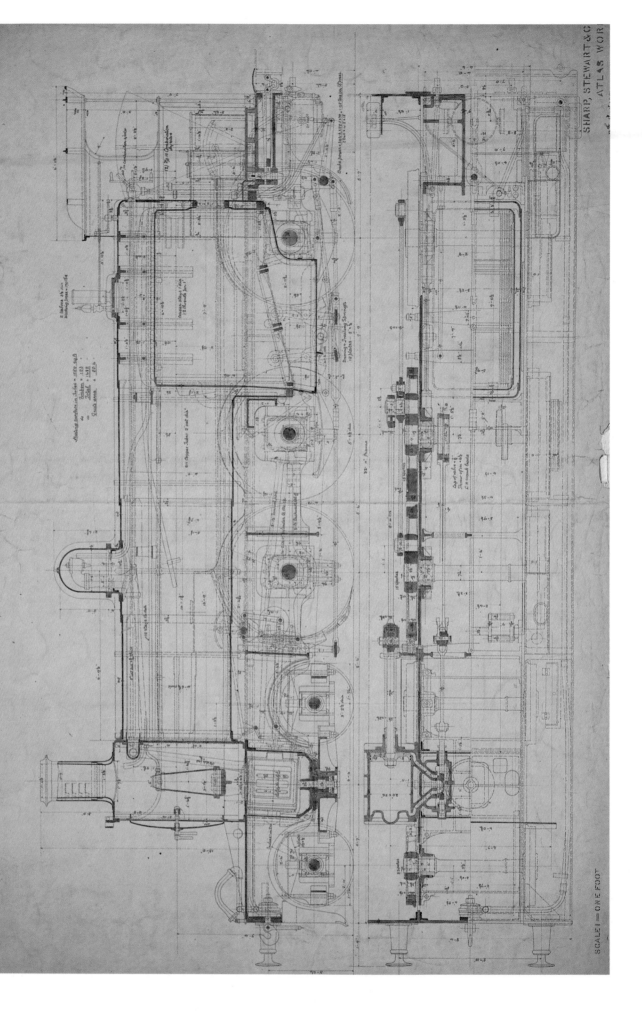

N⁰9981

SCALE ½ = ONE FOOT

SHARP, STEWART & C⁰

ATLAS WOR

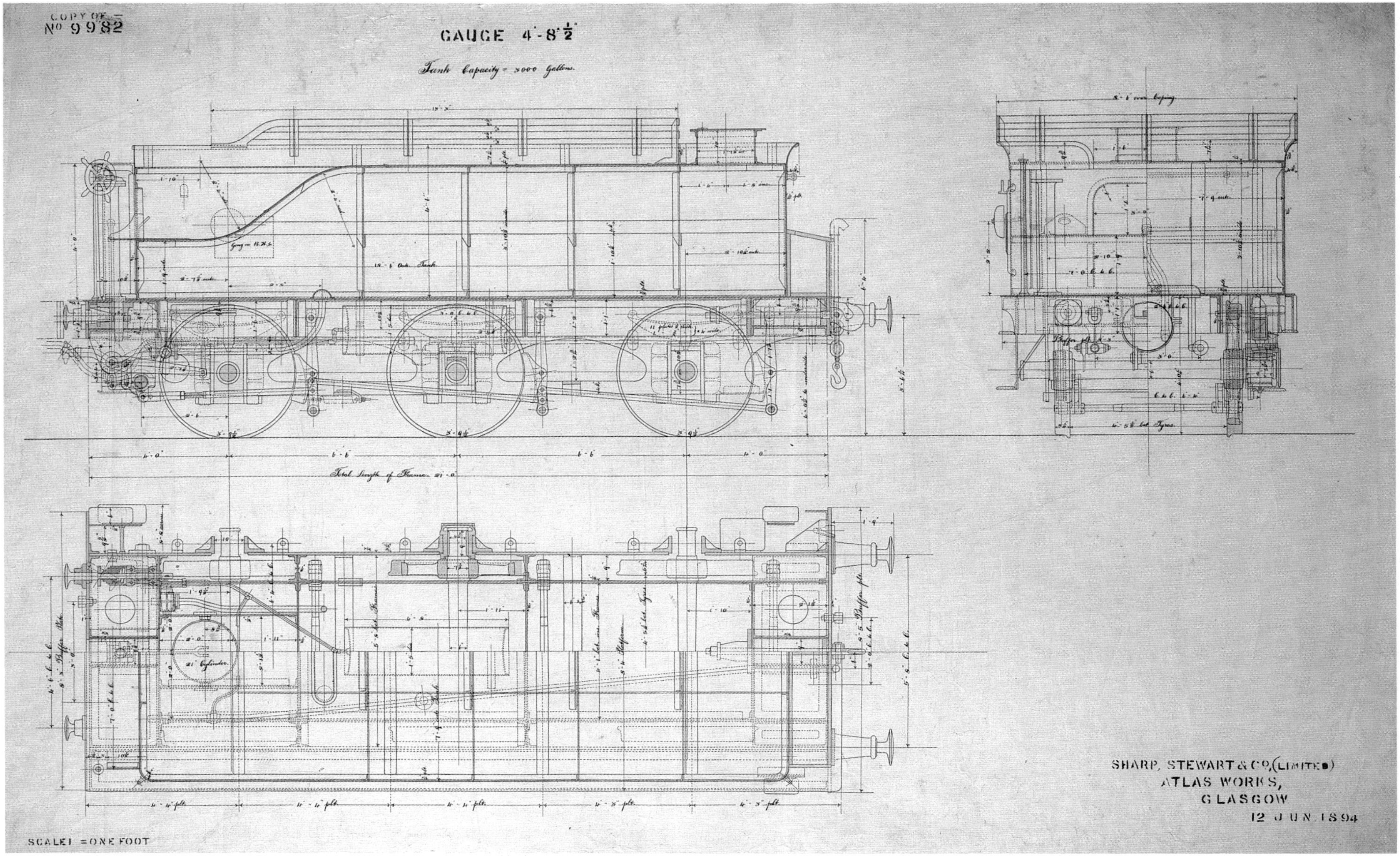
COPY OF
No 9982
GAUGE 4'-8½"
Tank Capacity = 3000 Gallons.
Total Length of Frame 21'-0"
SHARP, STEWART & Co (LIMITED)
ATLAS WORKS,
GLASGOW
12 JUN 1894
SCALE 1" = ONE FOOT

Historic significance, rather than strong colour, merits without question the inclusion of these drawings — both of locomotive and tender. The 'Jones Goods' introduced on the Highland Railway in 1894 was Britain's first 4-6-0.

Right:

Amongst my very few black-and-white photographs is this shot of Hawksworth GWR 'County' class 4-6-0 No 1020, *County of Monmouth* **at home at Bristol St Philips Marsh (82B) on 26 January 1963. Although superficially 'another Great Western 4-6-0', the 'Counties', with a new and larger boiler, owed a great deal to the Stanier boiler on the LMS '8F' 2-8-0. No 1020 has the double chimney fitted to most of the class. She was withdrawn from Swindon (82C) just over a year later.** *Author*

Below right:

'Modified Hall' No 6982 *Melmerby Hall,* **with Bristol Bath Road (82A) shedplate, at Bristol St Philips Marsh on 26 January 1963. After closure of St Philips Marsh, No 6982 was transferred to the former LMS shed at Bristol Barrow Road and withdrawn therefrom in August 1964.** *Author*

final chapter, the BR Standard classes, included two more 4-6-0s, of power-classification '4MT' and '5MT', the latter being generally regarded as essentially a 'Black Five' in BR guise. Stanier's recognition of the worth of the 4-6-0, as manifested in his rebuilt 'Scot' and 'Patriot', and his 'Jubilee' and 'Black Five', earns him a place alongside Churchward, than which there is no higher accolade.

I noted earlier some of the 4-6-0s that were captured in my lens when my photo-mission began.

It was my good fortune to have colour film in my trusty Voigtlander. Likewise it would be tedious in the extreme to list all the 4-6-0 photographs that I took. Suffice it to say that they appeared almost wherever I went. Not one page of my photo catalogue is bereft of an entry of this wheel-arrangement. They were there, right to the end: right to that moment of utter desolation as I slunk silently away from Rose Grove on 31 July 1968. It was the end of steam; but mercifully not the end of the 4-6-0.

CHAPTER FIVE

2-8-0

In a book devoted to the final years of working British steam, in which photographs albeit previously unpublished predominate, there is a certain inevitability about the choice of locomotive types, classes and wheel-arrangements which will feature. When the chapters of the book are dedicated to wheel-arrangements rather than individual classes, then the heading at the top of this page selects itself.

Not infrequently is one asked to nominate one's choice of 'favourite locomotive'. My routine answer is the GWR 'Castles': not a particularly surprising or imaginative answer, any more than would be the nomination of Beethoven as one's 'favourite composer'. Another, more selective, answer to the question sometimes sees me nominating the Urie 'S15': perhaps because their survival into the final five years of steam ensured that, as a very late arrival on the scene with my camera, my emotions were stirred by the sight of a genuine Pre-Grouping engine at this late hour. Contemplation of the subject of 'favourite class' caused me, in my last book, to soliloquise on my predeliction for the LNWR 'Super D' 0-8-0s, notwithstanding that I never actually saw one in steam on BR tracks. My geographical movements, too, were not conducive to the creation of opportunities to photograph those other splendid survivors, from the North Eastern Railway, the Raven 0-8-0s. However, to my list of 'favourite classes' which were still around at the beginning of the 1960s, and which I was — just — fortunate enough to see, were two classes of 2-8-0, which, whilst numerically tiny, not only survived, but also generated affection and created interest by their singularity. I refer to the GWR Churchward '47xx' 2-8-0s, and the S&DJR '7Fs' of the same wheel-arrangement.

One of the first words of this chapter was 'inevitability', so it is only a matter of time before the Stanier '8F' achieves its first mention in this chapter. Stanier's Swindon heritage itself prompts the making of the point that the Great Western was the first to introduce the 2-8-0 on to a British railway, when Churchward's '28xx' prototype, number 97, emerged from Swindon Works in 1903. Quantity production of these very fine engines began in 1905, originally in the glory of full passenger livery, polished brass and copper work. No greater contrast could be envisaged as between those halcyon days and the nether end of GW steam, when the few survivors of the derived Collett locomotives clanked out their final hours in a state of physical appearance, dereliction and mechanical neglect that was not surpassed in my experience by any other class on BR. The management of Western Region in 1965 seemed determined to spite the heritage of which they were, or should have been, the proud inheritors.

Whilst the '28xx' class had once sported with pride the livery of elegance to which I have referred, no such glamour ever attended the final British manifestation of 2-8-0, the Riddles WD 'Austerity', born in wartime. However, the lack of the visual appendages of pride and *élan* were certainly not matched by lack of appreciation of the mechanical attributes of these engines. In that the major part of the revenue-earning capacity of the northern railways was freight based, it was appropriate that the majority of the Riddles engines spent their lives in the northern part of the kingdom. When, as a politician, I am asked the puerile question 'would you like to have been Chairman of British Rail?' the one feature of recent rail policy that rankles more than any other and which one might have fought to avoid, is the deliberate policy of divesting the system of its freight traffic in the last few years: that is a policy that should not have been allowed to have been pursued. Please accept my apologies for

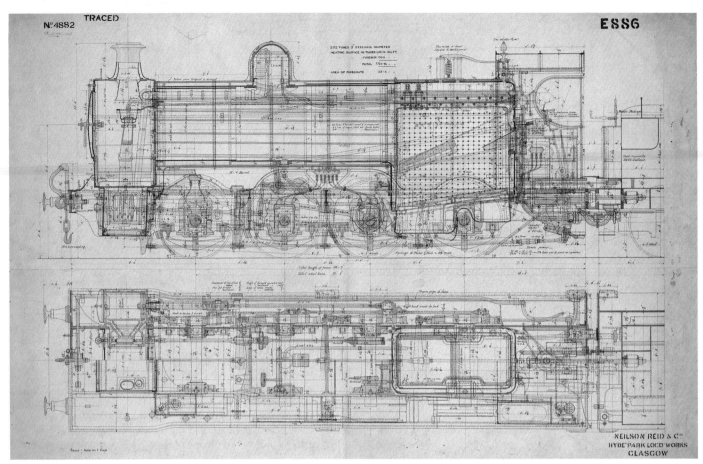

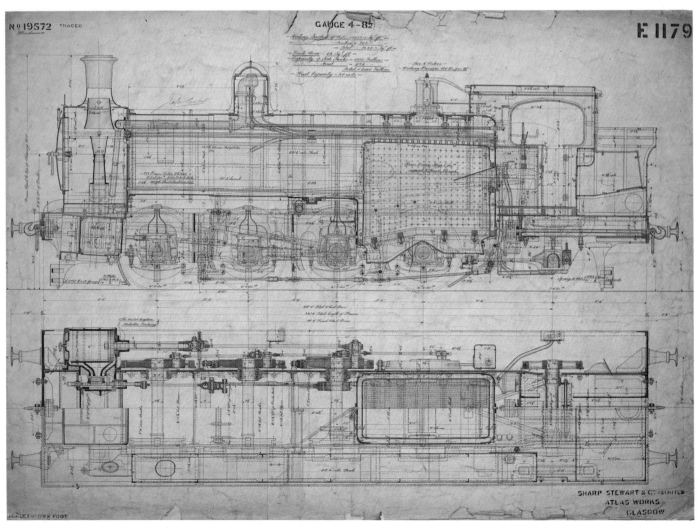

80

Top left:
Whilst strictly this drawing of an 0-8-0 does not in its wheel-arrangement match the chapter heading, there is no doubt of the close relationship, as explained in the extrapolation of Webb's LNWR 0-8-0 of Class B into Whale's conversion thereof into the 2-8-0 of Class E in 1904. Some two years earlier, on a drawing dated 11 July 1902, we see here a Neilson Reid 0-8-0 for the Barry Railway.

Left:
Even earlier, in 1901, Sharp Stewart built three 0-8-2Ts for the Port Talbot Railway. Two were withdrawn long before Nationalisation, in 1926 and 1935. One, GWR/BR No 1358, survived into BR ownership, to be withdrawn in 1948. It seems probable that the experience with eight-coupled locomotives, of two South Wales railways, was known to the GWR under Churchward who became the first to introduce the 2-8-0 heavy freight class; eight-coupled tank-engines were synonymous, in steam days, with South Wales.

Above:
On 29 May 1986, I visited Ivo Peters at his Bath home: on 28 June 1964, I had managed my one and only visit to Bath Green Park Shed, where S&D '7F' 2-8-0 No 53809 lay alongside the depot with a backdrop of Bath's terraced houses. One of the two members of this small, distinctive and very well-known class to survive into preservation, 53809 was built by Robert Stephenson to the design of Henry Fowler. Ivo Peters' superb photography of the Somerset & Dorset has immortalised the engines, with their 4ft 8½in driving wheels. No 53809 and the other 10 '7Fs' will always be part of the memory of an unforgettable railway, quintessentially through the lens of Ivo Peters' camera.

digressing from the subject in hand and for straying into the realm of railway politics; but a chapter on the 2-8-0 is inevitably a chapter about rail freight, and the condition of our 2-8-0s at the end of steam seems now, in retrospect, to have been a precursor of the railway management-of-the-day's attitude to freight traffic, its potential and its problems. What a depressingly classic example of matching the customer service to the perceived needs of the provider of the service, rather than vice versa. Local goods yards, local service, part-loads, all on rail; all gone, gone to the roads to the eternal discredit of politicians and management of the last generation.

In the period leading up to World War 1, the proportion of total revenue derived from freight traffic, on railways such as the Caledonian, North British, London & North Western and Lancashire & Yorkshire, was about 60%. On the Midland and North Eastern it was nearer 70%, which figure itself was indeed approached by the Great Central, with its intensive mineral traffic; in 1912 the GCR's freight revenue was 69.5% of its total from passenger, mail and freight. Thus the last of the 2-8-0s to which I can refer in the knowledge that they were still around in steam's final years, are the LNER derivatives of those splendid Robinson Great Central engines, the excellent design of which was adopted for war service by the Railway Operating Division (ROD) of the British Army. Perhaps, therefore, this is the appropriate point at which to list the 2-8-0s that I was able to photograph between the end of 1962 and the end of BR steam.

Class	First sighting		Loco number	Location	Allocation
'8F'	Nov	1962	48467	Luton	Kettering
'47xx'	Jan	1963	4700	Bristol St Philips Marsh	Withdrawn
WD 'Austerity'	March	1963	90154	King's Cross Top Shed	Peterborough New England
'28xx'	April	1963	3829	Acton	St Philips Marsh*
'01'	July	1963	63872	Peterborough New England	March
'04/8'	Feb	1964	63653	March	Frodingham
'7F' (S&DJR)	June	1964	53809	Bath Green Park	Bath Green Park

*Transferred to Croes Newydd that month.

Below:

A 'Military Mary': one of 30 new engines purchased by the LNWR directly from the Ministry of Munitions, classified 'MM' and thus earning the nickname, donated by their enginemen. Although intended by the Ministry for service on the Western Front, the war was over by the time the batch were completed — all but one by the North British Locomotive Co — and thus, in 1919, Crewe acquired them as 'mint' engines. Some historians claim that the LNWR bought them cheaply for their tenders; certainly some of the tenders, subsequently used by the LNWR/LMS behind the 'Claughtons', outlasted the locomotives, which the LMS sold to Armstrong Whitworth and Company in August 1927. (These engines were reconditioned, attached to new tenders and exported.) Delivery delays caused numbering problems and at one stage they were numbered in the 2800 series; indeed like their GWR '28xx' counterparts the Robinson Great Central 2-8-0s, of which the 'Military Marys' were only a minor modification, were one of the best large class of this wheel-arrangement to run on Britain's railways. The main difference between the standard GC engines and the ROD derivations was the Westinghouse brake, clearly visible here on one of the LNWR engines working an up freight at Hest Bank.

Unsurprisingly my most frequent 2-8-0 sightings were Stanier '8Fs' which, with the great man's 'Black Fives' were steam's final survivors at Lostock Hall, Rose Grove and Carnforth. They were widespread throughout the LMS system in England and Wales. The antecedence of the 2-8-0 on the LMS cannot really be traced back through the constituent companies, as can be done with other wheel-arrangements. The LNWR, Caledonian and L&Y all built 0-8-0s for mineral and heavy freight work, whilst the Midland with its small-engine policy, had four, six and (one) ten-coupled locomotives, but no eight-coupled engines. When Whale succeeded Webb on the LNWR he manifested his dislike of the front-end overhang of the latter's 'B' class 0-8-0 by experimentally converting one of the locomotives into a 2-8-0 by the addition of a pony truck. It was a reasonably successful experiment: 26 of the 'B' class were converted, and were designated Class E. A further 10 'B' class were similarly converted (see page 90) but were also given bigger boilers, and designated Class F. The LNWR conversions are

excellently documented by Edward Talbot in his *magnum opus LNWR Engines*. The LNWR was approaching the end of its independent existence in 1919 when the railway bought 30 2-8-0s, built by the North British Locomotive Company for the ROD for service on the Western Front. Before they were sent to France, the war ended, so the locomotives arrived on the LNWR as new engines. They were classified as 'MM', due to their having been ordered by the Ministry of Munitions. They earned the nickname of 'Military Marys' by the enginemen. Thus it is reasonable to claim that, as the 'E' and 'F' class 2-8-0s were converted 0-8-0s, and as the NBL/ROD/MM 2-8-0s were not an LNWR design, there was in fact no original 2-8-0 design, either on the LMS or on any of its constituent companies, before Stanier's '8F'.

Having mentioned the widespread allocation of the '8Fs', and the fact that they constituted easily my most frequently-sighted example of this wheel-arrangement, it has taken the investigation into my own photographs occasioned by this book to cause me for the first time to list the individual members of the class that I photographed. The inclusion of this list here illustrates the widespread presence of Stanier's engines even in their last six years; and also how far some of them strayed from their home base. From that first sighting of 48467 in November 1962, I have compiled my list in numerical rather than in chronological order.

Locomotive number	Date and location of photograph		MPD at date of photograph		Date of withdrawal
48012	9.09.66	Derby	5D	Stoke	April '68
48018	9.09.66	Derby	5D	Stoke	Oct '67
48018	9.03.67	Stoke-on-Trent	5D	Stoke	Oct '67
48027	4.63	Wellingborough	15A	Wellingborough	Mar '65
48036	9.08.67	Lostock Hall	8E	Northwich	Mar '68
48060	10.08.67	Speke Junction	8C	Speke Junction	April '68
48060	28.06.68	Speke Junction	8C	Speke Junction	
48062	25.06.68	Lancaster and Carnforth	10F	Rose Grove	Aug '68
48104	4.02.64	March	55A	Leeds Holbeck	July '67
48110	22.08.67	Stoke-on-Trent	5D	Stoke	June '67
48115	4.06.68	Rose Grove	10F	Rose Grove	July '67
48118	1.04.64	Cheadle Heath	8E	Northwich	June '66
48128	22.08.67	Stoke-on-Trent	5D	Stoke	June '67
48131	22.08.67	Stoke-on-Trent	5D	Stoke	June '67
48159	6.06.65	Southall	55D	Royston	Mar '67
48162	10.12.65	Rose Grove	55D	Royston	July '67
48163	19.09.65	Birkenhead	8C	Speke Junction	June '67
48163	3.10.65	Birkenhead	8C	Speke Junction	June '67
48166	25.07.67	Mirfield	9K	Bolton	Oct '67
48167	4.06.68	Rose Grove	10F	Rose Grove	Aug '68
48167	25.06.68	Carnforth	10F	Rose Grove	Aug '68
48206	5.63	Coventry	2B	Nuneaton	May '68
48214	10.08.67	Manchester Victoria	9H	Patricroft	Nov '67
48225	9.09.66	Derby	16E	Kirkby	Oct '66
48247	4.06.68	Rose Grove	10F	Rose Grove	Aug '68
48253	7.05.66	Birkenhead	6A	Chester	Aug '68
48253	4.06.68	Farington and Lostock Hall	10D	Lostock Hall	
48260	4.64	Plumbley	8H	Birkenhead	Nov '65
48261	10.12.65	Rose Grove	8F	Springs Branch Wigan	Aug '67
48270	9.09.66	Derby	16B	Annesley	Dec '66
48278	4.06.68	Rose Grove	10F	Rose Grove	Aug '68
48293	4.06.68	Rose Grove and Burnley	10D	Lostock Hall	June '68
48307	9.08.67	Lostock Hall	10D	Lostock Hall	Mar '68
48314	24.12.64	Feltham	16A	Toton	Dec '65
48317	21.12.67	Trafford Park	9E	Trafford Park	Mar '68
48335	4.06.68	Lostock Hall	10D	Lostock Hall	April '68
48336	6.06.64	Woodford Halse	1G	Woodford Halse	Dec '67
48340	31.07.68	Mintholme	10F	Rose Grove	Aug '68
48345	4.09.65	Birkenhead	6B	Mold Junction	Mar '68
48348	31.07.68	Rose Grove	10F	Rose Grove	Aug '68
48351	26.07.67	Speke Junction	5B	Crewe South	Jan '68
48367	9.09.66	Burton-on-Trent	16F	Burton	Sept '66
48386	10.12.65	Rose Grove	10F	Rose Grove	Aug '67
48393	31.07.68	Mintholme	10F	Rose Grove	Aug '68

Locomotive number	Date and location of photograph		MPD at date of photograph		Date of withdrawal
48395	9.09.66	Burton-on-Trent	16E	Kirkby	Sept '67
48402	18.07.66	Stourbridge	2B	Oxley	Dec '67
48410	4.06.68	Rose Grove	10F	Rose Grove	Aug '68
48423	8.67	Lostock Hall	10F	Rose Grove	
48423	4.06.68	Rose Grove	10F	Rose Grove	Aug '68
48423	31.07.68	Rose Grove	10F	Rose Grove	
48425	8.08.65	Birkenhead	8C	Speke Junction	Oct '67
48435	10.03.63	Tring	1A	Willesden	May '67
48440	3.63	Willesden	2E	Northampton	Feb '67
48448	4.06.68	Rose Grove	10F	Rose Grove	July '67
48451	2.12.64	Warrington	8B	Warrington	May '68
48460	1.63	Bristol St Philips Marsh	84F	Stourbridge	Sept '67
48467	11.62	Luton	15B	Kettering	June '68
48471	10.08.67	Manchester Victoria	9D	Newton Heath	May '68
48476	26.07.67	Speke Junction	8C	Speke Junction	Aug '68
48476	31.07.68	Lostock Hall	10D	Lostock Hall	
48493	8.08.65	Birkenhead	8C	Speke Junction	Aug '68
48493	31.07.68	Padiham	10F	Rose Grove	
48505	7.05.66	Birkenhead	5B	Crewe South	Oct '67
48507	9.03.67	Stockport	9B	Stockport	Mar '68
48511	6.08.65	Preston	9K	Bolton	July '66
48519	4.06.68	Lostock Hall Junction and Burnley Central	10F	Rose Grove	Aug '68
48522	4.09.65	Birkenhead	2F	Bescot	Aug '67
48546	4.06.68	Lostock Hall	10D	Lostock Hall	July '68
48546	25.06.68	Lostock Hall	10D	Lostock Hall	
48613	5.03.65	Patricroft	9F	Heaton Mersey	July '67
48631	10.03.67	Stockport	8E	Northwich	Feb '68
48646	4.06.68	Lostock Hall	10D	Lostock Hall	June '68
48652	25.06.68	Bolton	9K	Bolton	June '68
48655	6.03.65	Crewe	6B	Mold Junction	Aug '67
48662	17.07.65	Didcot	16F	Burton	Nov '66
48664	10.12.65	Rose Grove	55C	Farnley Junction	Oct '67
48665	31.07.68	Mintholme	10F	Rose Grove	Aug '68
48666	4.06.68	Mintholme	10F	Rose Grove	Aug '68
48666	31.07.68	Rose Grove	10F	Rose Grove	
48669	9.09.66	Banbury	2A	Tyseley	Oct '67
48673	8.67	Stockport	9B	Stockport	Oct '67
48674	26.07.67	Speke Junction	8C	Speke Junction	Dec '67
48715	4.06.68	Rose Grove	10F	Rose Grove	Aug '68
48717	9.03.67	Stockport	8E	Northwich	April '67
48720	25.06.68	Bolton	9K	Bolton	June '68
48737	28.06.64	Bath Green Park	82F	Bath Green Park	May '65
48752	18.07.66	Stourbridge	2B	Oxley	Aug '68
48754	23.06.63	Tring Cutting	2A	Rugby*	June '67
48754	4.02.64	March	1F	Rugby*	
48763	21.12.67	Trafford Park	9E	Trafford Park	April '68
48764	9.08.67	Lostock Hall	8F	Springs Branch Wigan	Dec '67
48765	25.06.68	Carnforth (or Lostock Hall)	10D	Lostock Hall	Aug '68
48773†	25.06.68	Bolton	9K	Bolton	Aug '68
48775	25.06.68	Burnden Junction Bolton	9H	Patricroft	Aug '68

Notes:
*Rugby's shed code was changed from 2A to 1F on 9.09.63.
†Preserved.

Right:
With two months left before the end of steam, Stanier '8Fs' were penned into their final bolt-holes at Carnforth, Lostock Hall and Rose Grove. The West Box at Rose Grove provides a prominent backdrop to No 48423, awaiting the road with a load of pulverised coal for Padiham power station, visible in the top right background and reached via the steeply-graded Padiham branch. No money 'wasted' now, on locomotive cleaning . . . it is 4 June 1968.

the tender away with considerable violence, only for the train to push it back into contact. The result was a brutal, bucking movement between engine and tender, usually at about 80 cycles/min, which made the enginemen's position unenviable and, if continued for any length of time, left the footplate knee-deep in coal 'jiggered' from the tender. There were only three possible ways of dealing with this purgatory: keep a breath of steam and run in front of the train (not practicable on long falling gradients); screw the tender handbrake on hard (not effective except on easy gradients) or grin and bear it. Needless to say, it was usually a case of the latter!'

The moral of this tale, insofar as it relates to non-Stanier modifications, would seem to be 'leave well alone', for in reality the '8F' 2-8-0 was a masterpiece of reliability, that could be, and very frequently was, mercilessly flogged. In spite of this, their maintenance costs were reasonable and they gave the operating department little cause for concern, and much satisfaction. Indeed, there was little compunction in pressing the class into use on summer excursions and relief trains (when there was no need for train heating), and their use *in extremis* on express passenger duty was by no means unknown.

In the penultimate sentence before the list I compiled of my photographs of '8Fs', there are these words . . . 'how far some of them strayed from their home base'. My reference was to, shall we say, Toton engines at Feltham; but many '8Fs' went overseas, whilst 23 never reached their destinations, being lost at sea during World War 2. '8Fs' were shipped far and wide. Twenty North British Locomotive Co (NBL) engines reached Turkey*; others served with British Army units in Iran and on railways in Egypt, Palestine and Lebanon. Some served in Italy. In addition to the engines built by NBL and Beyer Peacock, three other British railway companies (GWR, LNER and SR) built '8Fs' at Ashford, Brighton, Eastleigh, Swindon, Darlington and Doncaster, as well as at the LMS's own works at Crewe and Horwich. Indeed the LNER ordered 68 for its own use, designating them as Class O6. In the

*25 were originally shipped of which seven were lost at sea; two were subsequently sent.

Right:
LNWR 4-cylinder compound Class E 2-8-0 No 18; built at Crewe in 1902 as a Class B 0-8-0, she was one of 26 thus rebuilt and redesignated by Whale from the original Webb engines. The wheels are from a '17in coal engine'. Many of the converted 'E' class were rebuilt again, to Class 'G1', but No 18 was not; she was withdrawn in April 1928. As with the 'Bill Bailey' 4-6-0s, these engines rarely attract much attention, but have always interested me — thus my choice for inclusion here. (See page 82.)

Below right:
Ten Class B 0-8-0s were converted more radically than by the sole addition of the pony-truck to make them into 2-8-0s. They were given larger boilers, of the same diameter as Whale's 'Precursor' and 'Experiment' classes. These engines were designated Class F. No 9614 seen here in a rather smudged picture, was originally built at Crewe in May 1903; rebuilt as Class F in May 1906; and withdrawn in December 1928. Notes on the NRM file indicate this photograph was taken at Shrewsbury. (See page 82.)

Below:
'A Good Big-un': Robinson Great Central Class 8K 2-8-0 No 352, subsequently LNER Class O4/1. Of a class introduced in 1911, No 352, built at Gorton in August 1912, was withdrawn, as BR No 63640, in May 1959. Compare the finish and condition of this engine with the ex-ROD locomotive on page 98 .

light of prewar contention between the Streamliners of the LMS and LNER on the West and East Coast main lines, war indeed succeeded in submerging railway rivalry. The last active member of the class, other than preserved engines, was still working, at Erzinçan in Turkey, in September 1986, although officially steam working in that country was eliminated at the end of 1985.

There can be few similarities between the locomotive policies of the Midland Railway and of British Rail. One, however, is the absence of the design and construction of eight-coupled loco-motives. Indeed, it was the success of the '8F', and the large numbers built, that relieved Riddles and his team of the need to incorporate an eight-coupled machine amongst the BR Standard classes. It must not, however, be overlooked that Riddles himself fathered the last of the British-built 2-8-0s, his WD 'Austerity'. Before turning to this, the final class of this wheel-arrangement to be built in Britain for our home railways, it is relevant to say a few words about one other class of 2-8-0 to run on British metals, and which takes its place chronologically between the Stanier '8F' and the Riddles 'Austerity'. I refer to the USA 'S160' class.

As may be observed from the table below, the total number of 'S160s' far outstripped all the other classes of 2-8-0 listed. Almost all were built in the four years 1942-45, by the American 'Big Three' of Alco, Baldwin and Lima. Apparently, the design was considered, even in the United States, to be somewhat indelicate: high 'skirt', visible 'parts' and an appearance of being 'stripped for action' earning the 'S160' the nickname of a notorious lady of the day.

The class was one of the standard designs developed by the US Army for service worldwide, and were intended for use mainly in Europe. They complied with the British as well as the Continental European gauges. GWR, LMS, LNER and SR all had 'S160s' in service, although the SR locomotives were later transferred to the GWR.

The story of the American 2-8-0s has not been the subject of much interest, but such details as were recorded make an unusual episode in Britain's railway story. All the engines were, on arrival, passed through works for adjustments before being put into traffic. Soon there were more than enough and the later arrivals were put into store, very many in South Wales, prior to shipment to the Continent, starting in late 1944. The 'S160s' went far beyond Europe, their destinations including Korea and China, where at least 25 were sent. However, it is the influence of the 'S160' on subsequent British practice, rather than intrinsic interest in an American-designed and built locomotive, that merits mention of the class here.

At the outbreak of World War 2, Robin Riddles was asked to take charge of and form a Directorate of Transportation Equipment for the Ministry of Supply, whilst H. G. Ivatt, prior to the war actually breaking out, was also engaged on War Office work, albeit for a new tank — the tracked/fighting type, not an engine! Thus were two senior members of Stanier's LMS team working alongside each other. Their arrival on War Office duty perhaps predetermined the outcome of the marriage of LMS standardisation experience with wartime conditions of material shortages and concentration on performance rather than style. To these factors had to be added the need for locomotives to work overseas on track, with fuel and in conditions calling for rugged reliability in the hands of crews and of fitters, probably somewhat less refined than Top Link men from Camden, Crewe or Polmadie . . . Thus was conceived the 'Austerity' 2-8-0.

A glance at the chart below shows the similarity, in certain detail, of the 'vital statistics' of the LMS '8F', the US 'S160' and the Riddles 'Austerity' 2-8-0. The first 'Austerity' 2-8-0 was handed over to the Ministry of Supply on 16 January

The 2-8-0 on Britain's Railways: Some Comparisons

	'28xx'	'04/1'	'7F'	'47xx'	'8F'	'S160'	WD 'Austerity'	'O1' (g)
Railway/Operator	GWR	GCR	S&DJR (c)	GWR	LMS	USA/TC	WD/BR	LNER
Designer	Churchward	Robinson	Fowler	Churchward	Stanier	Maj J. W. Marsh	Riddles	Thompson
Date Introduced	1903	1911	1914	1919	1935	1942 (e)	1943	1944
Number Built	167 (a)	130 (b)	11	9	852 (d)	2,120 (f)	935	30
Coupled Wheel Diameter	4ft 7½in	4ft 8in	4ft 8½in	5ft 8in	4ft 8½in	4ft 9in	4ft 8½in	4ft 8in
Boiler Pressure (lb-sq in)	225	180	190	225	225	225	225	225
Tractive Effort (lb)	25,380	31,325	35,295	30,460	32,440	31,500	34,215	35,520

Notes:
(a) Total includes the later-built Collett locomotives.
(b) Many more built, by outside firms, after class was adopted in World War 1 and used by Railway Operating Department (ROD).
(c) Midland Railway design.
(d) 666 in service in UK: remainder shipped overseas but not returned.
(e) Date first in service in UK, being date of first construction also.
(f) Total built: not all came to Britain.
(g) Rebuilds of GCR locomotives.

Above:
Churchward (or Collett) '28xx', lower-quadrant semaphore signals, water-columns, loose-coupled freights — surely they would last forever. From a basic design introduced in 1903, these GWR heavy freight engines were matched against much more recently designed locomotives by the newly-appointed Railway Executive in 1948, and emerged as their equal, and in some characteristics better. On 4 May 1963, No 3818 stops for water west of Reading General station.

Below:
By 30 June 1963 — the date on which this photograph was taken — most of the remaining GWR 2-8-0s were of the Collett '2884' class, scrapping of the earlier '28xx' class having commenced in 1958. No 2842, one of the original Churchward engines built between 1903 and 1919, stands forlorn and withdrawn at Southall shed.

Above:

Between 1938 and 1942, 83 more GWR 2-8-0s were constructed during Collett's time as CME. Numbered 2884-3866 and thus known as the '2884' class, they were merely a modernised version of Churchward's sound design and were most easily distinguished from their unmodified predecessors by their side-window cabs, outside steam pipes and short safety-valve bonnets. With 84E (Tyseley) shedplate, No 3829 awaits the road at Acton (Main Line) station in April 1963. Tyseley MPD was transferred to the London Midland Region and recoded '2A' in the BR reorganisation of 1963.

Right:

As engine sheds closed in the last year of steam, scores of '8Fs' were abandoned. Motions were removed to ensure that they did not require lubrication whilst being towed to the cutter's yard; tracks both around and in the sheds rusted. Here, at Stoke-on-Trent on 22 August 1967 is portrayed that scene of despair that we came to recognise, with impotence and misery. For the sheds and their motive power, life became death, as here with '8F' No 48131. Rumours circulated that 20 '8Fs' were cocooned in plastic as a strategic military reserve; but no such evidence has been forthcoming.

Above:
This broadside shot is of a Lima-built American 'S160' class 2-8-0 at Reading in 1943. The inter-relationship between the 'S160' and Riddles' WD 2-8-0 makes for a fascinating study, reminiscent of the rival claims of Hedley and Stephenson 130 years earlier as to which was the father of the steam locomotive itself. The 'S160s' began to roll off the American production lines at the end of 1942, whilst the first Riddles WD 2-8-0 entered service in June 1943. However, the design premise for the 'S160' was specified by the British Ministry of Supply — whose Director of Transportation Equipment was Robin Riddles himself.

1943. Compared with the recorded contemporary reaction to Bulleid's 'Q1', comment on the new locomotive was not unfavourable. *The Railway Gazette* of 10 September 1943 states 'Externally the new locomotives make a very good impression; their appearance is neat and not unduly characterised by economy features'. The article continues . . . 'the internal construction is on well-tried lines and it is not immediately obvious from the drawings where savings have been achieved in material and labour. Nevertheless these savings are substantial and a closer study of the details will show that many have been fabricated to eliminate, as far as possible, the use of steel castings and forgings'.

In the heat of wartime production, the manufacturers — North British and Vulcan Foundry — set new records in rapid locomotive construction. Until October 1944 all the 2-8-0s delivered from the manufacturers (some 450 at this time) were on loan to the railways in Britain, but from then onwards they were shipped to the Continent for use by the advancing British Army in France, Belgium and Holland, and on towards Germany. The 'Austerities' were built in the knowledge that they would need to be readily adaptable to 'foreign' conditions. The boiler could be converted to oil-burning without removal from the engine; whilst bolt-holes were provided in front of the engine for the easy attachment of cowcatchers for service in appropriate destinations.

Of the 935 'Austerity' 2-8-0s built, 733 found their way back to Britain for service on British Railways; only three of the class were not sent overseas, Nos 77223, 77369 and 79250. Brian Haresnape, as ever, provides much fascinating detail of the overseas adventures of the class in *Ivatt & Riddles*

Locomotives. In the light of the diligence and enthusiasm for tracing the history of each and every individual locomotive, one can only wonder what happened to No 79189. Built by Vulcan Foundry in 1944, she was one of 227 acquired by the Netherlands Railways, after departure from whom she 'disappeared': in wartime parlance, 'missing presumed lost'.

Back on British metals after duty abroad, the Riddles 2-8-0s settled down to a humdrum life: 'Austerity' locomotives in postwar austerity Britain. Whatever appeal they may have lacked for contemporary enthusiasts, they were entirely welcome to the hard-pressed foremen and shedmasters of the day. Not that these men were part of a concerted crescendo of uncritical acclaim; quite the reverse in fact. Running tests of the class, and their 2-10-0 cousins, were carried out on the former Glasgow & South Western line between Carlisle and Hurlford, utilising the former LMS Mobile Test Plant, from which emanated much criticism; as also followed the reports on the class after the 1948 interchange trials. In retrospect, the genesis of the criticism was related to the expectations and standards anticipated and obtained from prewar British locomotives of the highest quality, rather than of the 'rough' and utilitarian 'Austerities'. The fact is that in postwar service conditions, rather than on test by 'theoreticians', the class more than earned their corn and the respect of those who worked with them day in and day out.

With postwar labour shortages came growing disinclination for the hard, dirty work of the steam engine-shed. Thus the ease of maintenance which was a constructional *raison d'être* continued to be a factor much in their favour. Of the locomotives on BR, the first was withdrawn in 1959, but many continued in service almost up to the end of steam. Their main stamping ground, in their final years, was

Above:
By 1944, when the Thompson 'O1' rebuilds were introduced, with their 'B1' boilers, side window cab, Walschaerts valve-gear and raised running-plate, there was not much visual resemblance to the Robinson Great Central 2-8-0s from which this assorted 'class' was derived. Indeed, few better illustrations could be found of the rebuilding mania that beset the LNER in later years, from locomotives of its constituent companies. 'O1' No 63872 is reversed gently into the gloomy recess of New England Shed, Peterborough, on 7 July 1963. The 'O1s' were classified '8F' by British Railways.

Below:
Epitomising the condition of steam in those final years, and illustrating the uncompromisingly rugged appearance of these locomotives, is Riddles' 'Austerity' 2-8-0 No 90533, at Newton Heath MPD on 3 December 1964. Greater Manchester seemed often to provide me with better weather than the so-called 'sunny south'!

Above:

With the Great Central Railway's General Manager, Sir Sam Fay, as Director of Movements, War Office, it was perhaps not surprising that the Robinson GCR 2-8-0 was chosen as the standard freight engine for military railway operations in France in the later stages of World War 1. More than 500 of these first class locomotives were thus built by various contractors, mainly for use by the Railway Operating Division (ROD) of the British Army. After the war, these ROD engines returned; here number 3012, built by the North British Locomotive Company and purchased by the GWR in 1919, heads a freight near Patchway *circa* 1935. She was withdrawn, by BR, in May 1956.

in the north and northeast, appropriate in the world of mining and heavy industry, although my first photo-sightings were of New England engines Nos 90154 and 90269 at Top Shed, King's Cross, in March 1963. Twenty-four 'Austerities' survived until September 1967, less than a year before the end of steam, and of these six were at Sunderland (52G), seven at West Hartlepool (51C) and 11 at Normanton (55E), from which they were withdrawn that month. Having listed my '8F' photographs it would be over-egging the pudding to do likewise for the 'Austerities', although certain sightings linger in the memory.

Notwithstanding the emergence of the preservation era, with its proper appreciation of the need to save as wide a variety of locomotive classes as possible, and despite the fact that the very last WD 2-8-0, No 90682, was not withdrawn from Normanton Shed until late September 1967, not one of the 733 members of the class at work on BR was saved from the cutter's torch. Fortunately, however, the Swedish State Railways had acquired two of the 'Austerities' from the Netherlands Railways for use north of the Arctic circle. Stored for use in case of strategic emergency, one locomotive has survived, to be returned to the land of its birth, for preservation.

As mentioned earlier, the success and the large numbers of both Stanier '8F' and Riddles WD 'Austerity' 2-8-0s precluded the need for locomotives of this wheel-arrangement to be included amongst the British Standard steam locomotive classes built by the nationalised British Railways. This decision was most certainly *not* occasioned by the 2-8-0 being considered as unsuitable for modern freight, for it was indeed, with the sole exception of the '9F' 2-10-0, the final British manifestation of the heavy freight locomotive.

CHAPTER SIX

FOUR-COUPLED

Whereas the ten-coupled designs of all but two individual locomotives were manifestations of the final flowering of British steam design, the four-coupled machine dated quite literally from the dawn of the steam era. However, it would be misleading to assume that the phrase 'four-coupled' referred only to ancient and diminutive machines. Indeed it can perhaps be claimed that the variety of 'ancient and modern' in steam power could be found represented in the ranks of the two-axle drivers more completely than elsewhere. As this book relates primarily to the last five years of British steam, to my own photographs, and thus to those classes of locomotive that I was able to see and photograph, the point can be made from my memory.

To scour the records of the four-coupled locomotive classes (such as LNER Sentinels in Departmental service) still represented on the books of British Rail, at the beginning of 1963, would be a time-consuming task seeking an unimportant objective within an arbitrary time scale. Let memory suffice to illustrate the point about wide variety, as between the '0298' class 2-4-0WT with a tractive effort of 11,050lb, and, from a class of four-coupled locomotives introduced more than half a century later, the 'Schools' or 'V' class 4-4-0 with a tractive effort of 25,135lb. I was able to photograph an example of both classes within seven days; at Eastleigh Shed on 18 May 1963, and Beattie Well Tank No 30587 at Nine Elms on 25 May. In fact, the 'Schools' concerned was No 30934 *St Lawrence*, which had run down from Basingstoke to Eastleigh under her own steam. I claim that my photographs of her that day were the last colour photographs of an unpreserved four-coupled tender locomotive in steam on BR metals and the last colour photograph of a 'Schools' in steam on Southern metals.

Few people, whatever their prejudices and predilections (and railway enthusiasts are short of neither) would dispute that Maunsell's splendid

three-cylinder 4-4-0s were the most successful, as well as the most powerful and most modern, four-coupled locomotives ever to run in Britain. Whilst *City of Truro* can arguably claim a dramatic 'one-off' speed record, the prodigious feats of the 'Schools' in regular service with heavy trains, tight schedules and the discipline of interspersement with numerous electric trains on suburban tracks, were legion. Designed by Maunsell to meet the operational requirements of the day — greater route availability than the 'King Arthur' and 'Lord Nelson' classes of 4-6-0, and of intermediate power rating — the SR's CME produced the most powerful 4-4-0 ever to run in Europe. Maunsell's department used the valves, front-end design and cylinders (three not four) as on the 'Nelsons' and a shortened version of the boiler from the 'Arthurs'. The 40 locomotives of the class thus incorporated the best features of both the 4-6-0 designs. The demands of the Traffic Manager were for a locomotive to haul 400-ton trains at an average speed of 55mph. The 'Schools' met the specified speed, often with loads of 500 tons.

That day at Eastleigh reminded me how late in the day I had entered the ranks of those photographing steam's final years. After electrification of the Portsmouth route in 1936, the 'Schools' locomotives shedded at Fratton were transferred to Bournemouth and took over the working of some of the London expresses from the 'King Arthurs' at a time when this service was timetabled faster than ever before. I rarely heard a bad word spoken about the 'Schools'. When the Kent Coast lines, their last major preserve, were electrified, the class were dispersed from their previous bases of Bricklayers Arms, Dover, Ramsgate and St Leonards as the featureless EMUs took over. During what became their last year of service, they were allocated to the sheds at Nine Elms, Brighton, Basingstoke, Redhill and Guildford, from which two latter sheds they carried out some of their final passenger duties on

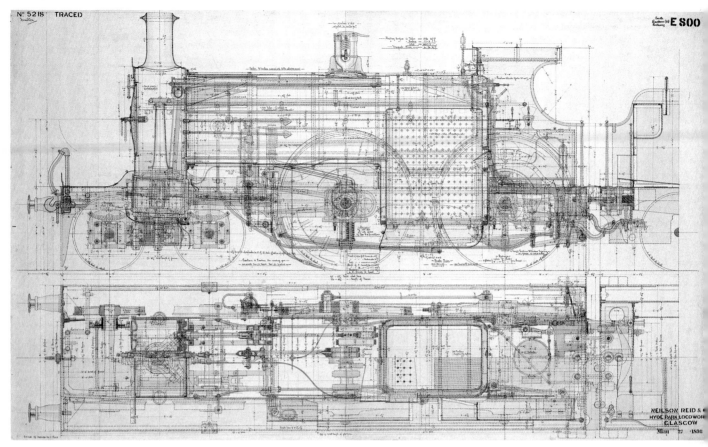

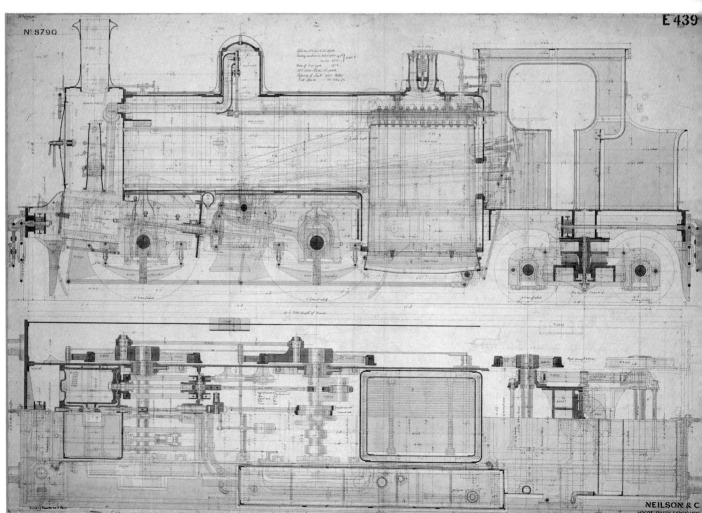

100

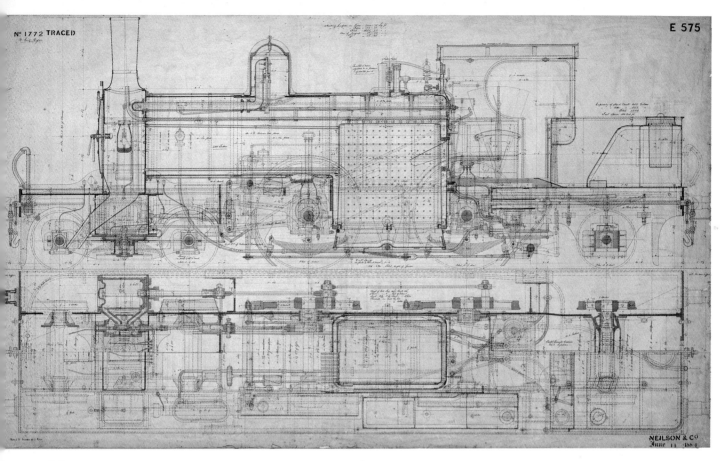

No 1772 TRACED

E 575

NEILSON & CO
June 11 1884

Top left:
Neilson Reid-built 4-4-0 for the South Eastern Railway. Drawing dated 27 May 1898. It bears little resemblance to Britain's last new class of 4-4-0, Maunsell's Southern Railway 'Schools' class, introduced 1930, many of which worked the former lines of the SER.

Left:
Neilson-built 0-4-4T, from a drawing dated 24 February 1875.

Above:
This drawing, dated 11 June 1884, will be easily recognisable to those who remember the final steam years of the Axminster-Lyme Regis branch, on which the three surviving Adams LSWR 4-4-2Ts were a magnet for photographers. Seventy-one engines were built between 1882-85. The original series were well tank locomotives with smaller, square rear splashers, whilst later members of the class had these splashers extended forward to provide small side-tanks for increased water supply.

---

the SECR Redhill to Reading line. With the exception of the three survivors — Nos 30925/6/8 — all but two were scrapped at Eastleigh or Ashford Works between March 1961 and March 1964. Nos 30902/21 were sold to Cohens, Kettering, and were cut up there in March 1964. I was fortunate indeed to see *St Lawrence* in steam that day, having only seen dead 'Schools' previously, namely Nos 30901 *Winchester*, 30911 *Dover*, 30915 *Brighton*, 30916 *Whitgift* and 30923 *Bradfield* dumped at Hove in February

1963. No 30911 was still at Hove when my camera and I were there on 5 May 1963.

Bradfield was lucky to be included amongst the 40 'Schools' after which the Maunsell class were named. 30923 was originally christened *Uppingham*, but the then headmaster, one Dr Owen, objected to what he deemed to be rather cheap publicity for his school. As an Old Uppinghamian myself — albeit not even a gleam in my parents' eyes at the time the locomotives were built — I have always nurtured a deep grievance against that Dr Owen for depriving my old school of inclusion amongst illustrious fellows — by membership of a locomotive class if not by educational company. Dr Owen's rather stuffy attitude to the Southern Railway's naming committee's efforts was doubtless looked at differently by the school after which No 30923 was named — *Bradfield*, of which another Dr Owen is an Old Boy.

But the tale of No 30923 has long aggravated me. In 1984 I was invited to deliver the speech at the dinner to terminate the quadringenary celebrations of the school. Some months prior to this auspicious event, I asked the Headmaster, Nick Bomford, for his permission for me to approach the Chairman of BR, Sir Robert Reid, with a view to repairing the 'damage' to railway/school relations, my ambition being to try to have a diesel or electric locomotive named *Uppingham*. Bob Reid rejected my request on what I felt frankly to be rather spurious grounds in the light of current BR naming policy. I was disappointed: not angry — after all who really *cares* about the names of diesel or electric locomotives,

101

Two North Eastern Railway 0-4-4 tank engines, of a wheel-arrangement used extensively in northeast England. Scant detail is available in the NRM Library, from which these pictures come. The official Darlington photograph *(top)* of No 1783 is probably one of William Worsdell's 'O' class; No 950 *(above)* as designed by Edward Fletcher. It is from the first 12 of a class built by Neilson's in 1874. With integrated sandboxes and splashers plus distinctive wheels. No 950 has a jaunty if somewhat rakish air. Although some Fletcher engines in original condition (he was NER Locomotive Superintendent from 1854-1883) lasted until 1929, it is the Worsdell and Raven designs on the NER which are best remembered.

when compared to the honour and glory of adorning an express passenger steam locomotive?

From such flights of fancy we should return to four-coupled locomotives. That day at Eastleigh when I saw 30934 in steam (having also seen her earlier the same day at Basingstoke) yielded other four-coupled Southern Region motive power. My records indicate that I also photographed 'B4' 0-4-0 tank No 30096, 'M7' 0-4-4 tank No 30251, 'O2' 0-4-4 tank No 30199, and restored 'T9' 4-4-0 No 120: quite a collection indeed, although most — but not No 120 — were dumped on the scrap lines, awaiting the cutter's torch.

For students of the classes of locomotives of individual designers, recent publications are a veritable treasure-trove of information. D. L. Bradley has written an excellent book, the first of three volumes devoted to the locomotives of the LSWR featuring the Adams classes. His chapter on the 'B4' 0-4-0T details the diverse career of these small but quite powerful little locomotives. The 'B4' I saw that overcast day at Eastleigh was originally LSWR No 96 *Normandy*. Built at Nine Elms in November 1893, she spent many years at Southampton Docks on

work for which a four-coupled wheelbase was essential. She received her BR number, 30096, in December 1950, received a second BR general repair and repaint in the mid-1950s, and was one of only two members of the class, and the last at that, to receive a third BR repair and repaint in July 1959. Born into the Victorian age, she was spruced up in time for Harold Macmillan's 'You've never had it so good'.

Many members of the class were lent, hired or sold and sometimes repurchased, by their various owners, LSWR/SR/BR, and No 30096 was no

Below:
Attributed to Stanier, but clearly not of his doing — in fact one of the LMS 0-4-4Ts, in reality a Midland design attributed to Lemon, but introduced after Stanier's arrival on the scene. In an era of change, little notice was taken of these locomotives, which, by the standard of longevity of this wheel-arrangement on other railways, soon passed from the scene. Note the non-standard chimney and prominent sandbox — very much a locomotive more akin to the 1890s than the 1930s. (See chart page 106.)

exception. However, she was one of the last active survivors in BR revenue-earning service, including a brief return to Southampton Docks at the end of 1960. When I saw her, dead, at Eastleigh on 18 May 1963 her fate seemed sealed, standing amidst condemned and rusting engines, although not officially withdrawn, the last of the class, until December. However, in December that year she was in fact, sold to a subsidiary of Corrall's, renamed *Corrall Queen*, and put back to work in Southampton at Dibbles Wharf. Final glory came in December 1972, when No 30096 was purchased by the Bulleid Preservation Society for £1,000, and taken by road to the Bluebell Railway for preservation; not bad for an engine that had cost £1,150 when built just 79 years earlier.

'O2' No 30199, adjacent to 30096, was another one-off sighting for me that day. Again D. L. Bradley provides excellent detailed histories of the individual members of another Adams four-coupled class, indeed even older than the 'B4s'. In latter years the 'O2s' became famous, and well-photographed, on the Isle of Wight. Much less was heard, or notice taken, of the members of the class that never crossed the Solent, of which No 199 was one. Ordered in a batch of 10 from Nine Elms Works, on 29 January 1890, No 199 was put into service the following year. She spent many years in the West Country, including time based at Wadebridge, working Okehampton and Bude services, and latterly at Exmouth Junction through World War 2 and beyond. She received her BR number, 30199, in September 1949, and with sister engine No 30225 became one of the two final 'O2' survivors, being finally withdrawn in December 1962. 'Survivors' seems indeed to be the correct word to describe both 30096 and 30199. Dead in my lens they may have been that day; but not in my memory, or in the words and photographs of D. L. Bradley's excellent book.

If the 'Schools' were the most illustrious four-coupled locomotives still in steam in 1963 — and my photographs that day were in spite of the fact that all were officially withdrawn by the end of 1962 — then the LSWR 'M7s' were amongst the most long-lived survivors of a class introduced in 1897 and still active at the time. Indeed it was to my pleasure and satisfaction that 'M7' No 30251 appeared in the background of one of my photographs of *Flying Scotsman* on shed at Eastleigh that day, 18 May 1963 (see plate 31 in *The Call of Steam*). My last photograph of an 'M7' was one of No 30111, dumped and left to rot outside Nine Elms Shed. She was rusting fast when I photographed her on 7 July 1964.

Another class of 0-4-4 tank engine at work on southern metals, well into the 1960s, were the Wainwright South Eastern & Chatham 'H' class locomotives, none of my photographs of which has previously appeared in any of my books. As with their near-contemporaries on the LSWR, the 'M7s',

the 'H' tanks were an outstanding example of the value for money represented by the steam engine to the railway company. Sixty years after their introduction in 1904, members of the class were still regularly employed on passenger services in the Sussex/Kent border areas. They survived on the non-electrified lines such as Three Bridges-East Grinstead, and observant discerning enthusiasts travelling on Brighton-Victoria trains could catch a glimpse of one of these veterans at the head of its train in the covered bay platform at Three Bridges. My first 'sighting' on 23 March 1963 was odd indeed, at an inaccessible and remote location west of Edenbridge, at the point where the former LBSCR Oxted to Tunbridge Wells line, in tunnel, emerges momentarily into the daylight as it passes under the SECR Redhill-Tonbridge line. No 31263 appeared fleetingly at this dimly-lit point. Some three weeks later I found myself at Tunbridge Wells West station, where No 31518 was awaiting departure at the head of the 16.00 train to Oxted. That same month saw me back at Tunbridge Wells West MPD, where Nos 31005, 31308, 31518 and 31544 were on shed (75F). Finally, on 13 July 1963, I photographed No 31542 at Stewarts Lane MPD. The early BR 'Lion' emblem had re-emerged but her builder's plate seemed long-removed. That day, incidentally, 'Schools' 4-4-0 No 30928, *Stowe*, in clean condition for preservation, was on Stewarts Lane Shed too. I was fortunate at such a late date to see six 'H' tanks, particularly as Kent was a most rare stamping-ground for me.

Everyone is a creature of his own environment. We all have our favourite locomotives and locations. We tend to learn more about those people, places and things that touch our lives or heighten our interest. Taking London as the hub, points

---

Top right:
Originally designed by W. Adams for the LSWR in 1891, 25 of these 0-4-0T dock shunters of Class B4 came into Southern Railway stock in 1923. By the winter of 1962/63 only three were left, of which No 30096 was one, seen here soon after withdrawal, at Eastleigh on 18 May 1963. She survived, via Corralls at Southampton, and now resides at the Bluebell Railway.

Right:
When new, in 1897, the first LSWR 'M7' 0-4-4Ts would doubtless have worked London suburban trains from Nine Elms Shed. Nearly 70 years later, one of the last survivors of Drummond's splendid machines, No 30111, stands forlorn, rusting but still distinctive and even haughty at Nine Elms on 7 July 1964. Twixt the premierships of Lord Salisbury and Harold Wilson, members of the class performed prodigious deeds, on LSWR main line trains between Exeter and Plymouth; on taxing London suburban duty; on semi-fasts on Alton and Portsmouth services; and latterly on branch-line work from Devon to Sussex, as well as on heavy empty stock trains into and out of Waterloo.

westwards, not eastwards, have been my *métier*. Thus the LSWR was and is a line that has crossed my path at many points in time and place, whilst, with the considerable exception of its Redhill to Reading line, the SECR was and still is almost a total blank in my arena of personal knowledge and experience. Thus my brief glimpses of 'H' class 0-4-4Ts were insufficient to enable me to claim any familiarity. One cannot help but be aware, however, from all those books about the 'Southern in Kent', 'Kent and its Branch Lines', etc that Wainwright's engines were the mainstay for many of those odd little services for almost 60 years.

Of the four-coupled locomotives about which to write, and which I never saw, the choice is endless. The name Stanier is rarely if ever associated with such wheel-arrangements, but his name is attached to two LMS locomotives, albeit neither his brainchild. In 1932, soon after his arrival on the scene, five 0-4-0 saddle-tanks were ordered; they are described in the Ian Allan *Locomotives and Locoshed Book* as 'Kitson design prepared to Stanier's requirements for LMS'. The other class attributed to the great man, but in reality the work of E. J. H. Lemon, were the 10 0-4-4Ts classified '2P' and also introduced in 1932. They have always seemed to me to be an anachronism, and in longevity never matched the 'H' or 'M7' machines of identical wheel-arrangement. Perhaps a glance at the vital statistics of these three 0-4-4Ts will suffice in a chapter whose permutations are endless, to show only how little had changed in 35 years in these vital statistics.

One of life's great conundra is the question of how to recognise one's opportunities. There were two periods in my life which, in retrospect, represent my 'wasted years' from the viewpoint of railway interest and particularly railway photography. One of these covers the school holidays from about 1946-1952. I can remember now cycling from home in Hove northwards to a bridge near one of the portals of Clayton tunnel on the London-Brighton main line, with a chum, Paul Balen, whom I have not seen for many years. We used to collect numbers on the 6-PUL, 6-PAN, 4-LAV and occasional 2-BIL units: and great were the exclamations on the appearance of a steam-hauled train. My ignorance of railway matters was almost total. Train journeys, except to and from school at the beginning and end of each term, were rare. Platform tickets at Hove, or Brighton, were my main means of entry into the railway world. Perhaps if pocket money permitted or resources for an 'excursion' were proffered, a train journey might be undertaken. Dimly I can recall Hove to West Worthing on a NOL, or Brighton to Lewes, without realising that a steam-hauled Brighton to Tonbridge or Oxted train was an available option. Had I but realised then that 4-4-0s of Class L or L1 could have been my motive power. It is too late now.

If 'L' and 'L1' 4-4-0s were a postwar option for quite a few years, then so too were the variations of MR and LMS 4-4-0s, including the famous 'Compounds'. However, this is a personal ramble, and although I may occasionally have seen those locomotives, no recollection remains — only a great gap. Nostalgia for events unknown and things unseen leaves me only with recriminations and feelings of utter certainty that what has gone, has gone. Of Great Central or North British 4-4-2Ts I knew nothing; likewise mysterious Pre-Grouping oddities like LNER Classes Y1, Y9, Z4 or Z5, to name but four. Of the four-coupled locomotives that I wish I had seen, perhaps Aspinall's 1889 Lancashire & Yorkshire 2-4-2Ts with Joy valve gear are amongst my greatest frustrations.

Apart from 'Schools', 'M7' and 'H', my sighting of four-coupled classes was restricted to that LSWR

0-4-4T	'M7'	'H'	'2P'
Date introduced	1897	1904	1932
Railway	LSWR	SECR	LMS
Designer	Drummond	Wainwright	Lemon/Stanier
Number built	105	66	10
Cylinders	18½in×26in	18in×26in	18in×26in
Pressure	175lb	160lb	160lb
Driving wheels	5ft 7in	5ft 6in	5ft 7in
Tractive effort	19,755lb	17,360lb	17,100lb
Last withdrawn	1964	1964	1962

Left:
The 0-4-4T wheel-arrangement was still to be seen at work, in the London area, in the 1960s. Far away from the metropolis, at one of Britain's shortest-lived railway outposts, stands North British 0-4-4T No 590 at Fort Augustus by Loch Ness. A visit here today is recommended for anyone tracing the remains of Britain's lesser-known railway lines.

Below:
The unusual bogie wheels earn this North British 4-4-0T, No 1404, its place here. Photographed at Causeway Head.

Bottom:
North British Railway 'Scott' class 4-4-0 No 422 *Kenilworth* at Dunfermline Upper.

Overleaf left:
One of the 'H' class 0-4-4Ts not fitted for push-and-pull working, No 31542, at Stewarts Lane depot on 13 July 1963. On the left, behind the engine, is Stewarts Lane crane: on the right, just visible, is Maunsell 'N' 2-6-0 No 31412, another SECR design.

Overleaf right:
All Maunsell's renowned 'Schools' 4-4-0s having been officially withdrawn by the end of 1962, it was with astonishment that I stumbled on No 30934 *St Lawrence* in steam and being prepared for duty, inside Basingstoke shed on 18 May 1963. Please excuse a poor photograph, justified by my extreme shortage of material of this most illustrious modern and powerful example of four-coupled steam.

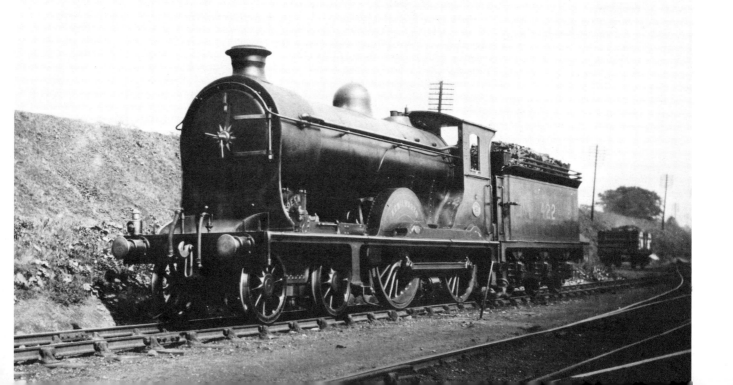

Between the Science Museum working drawings and my very few colour photographs of the handful of four-coupled locomotives still extant into the last five years of British steam, as illustrated in this book, lies virtually the visual history of the development of Britain's railways, and no attempt effectively to portray such a panorama could be attempted in one book, let alone one chapter. My choice, therefore, to span the gap between 'Rocket' and 'Schools' falls on the Midland Railway/LMS 4-4-0s, delightfully put into historic perspective by Maurice Earley's 1932 photograph of a Birmingham train setting out from Derby in charge of No 716.

'B4' No 30096 dead at Eastleigh on 18 May 1963, two of those three Beattie 2-4-0WTs at Nine Elms on 25 May 1963; and one or two dismal photographs of GWR '14xx' class 0-4-2Ts. I found No 1474 dead at Southall on 28 April 1963. These Collett locomotives belied their comparatively modern genesis. I suppose that the concept of a four-coupled tank engine was more 'ancient' than 'modern'; whilst the tall chimney accentuated rather the visual as opposed to the actual vintage of this class. Introduced in 1932 and originally designated '48xx' class, they were push-and-pull fitted, whilst those not so fitted were designated '58xx' class. Being small, they attracted little attention; not even a mention do

they rate in O. S. Nock's *The British Steam Railway Locomotive 1925-1965*.

The '14xxs' were scattered around the GWR and latterly Western Region. After nationalisation one or two found their way to other region's sheds — Neasden and Exmouth Junction to name but two, at which latter depot the final two survivors, Nos 1442 and 1450, ended their days, being withdrawn in May 1965. Both have survived into preservation.

How and why No 1474, the last of the class, returned to Southall I do not know. Its career well illustrates the nomadic existence of these little engines in their final years. Perhaps sheer nostalgia summoned 1474 'home' for she was a Southall (81C) engine up to October 1958 when she was transferred to Weymouth (71G). By April 1960 she was on the move again, this time to Slough (81B) for but a month before returning to Southall. Shuttlecock along the GWR main line appears to have been her lot: Southall back to Slough in January 1961; to Southall in June; then a year later back to Slough. Her penultimate move, in August 1963, was to Exeter St Davids (85C), her last reallocation taking place in May 1964, when she went to Gloucester Horton Road (85B). Four months later 1474 was withdrawn, stood for two months at the shed and was sold to and cut up by Birds at Morriston, Swansea, that December. In the cold mid-winter long, long ago . . .

CHAPTER SEVEN

4-6-2

From *The Great Bear* to *Duke of Gloucester*, 1908-1954, may indeed be less than half a century, but within that timespan is encompassed the full flowering of modern British express passenger steam locomotive history. That neither No 111 nor No 71000 was without its critics is indisputable. That little or nothing new remains to be written about either, or indeed about the Pacifics sandwiched between the British prototype and the ultimate manifestation thereof, is equally probable. Perhaps the only contribution I can make to a 'Parable of the Pacifics' is to seek to tabulate each separate class to run on Britain's railways. To claim this as an original tabulation would doubtless be inaccurate: my searches have not however revealed any such identical, or even similar juxtapositioning of *all* these locomotives. Indeed it was Simon Forty, Ian Allan's Publishing Director, who saw the chart in my chapter

on the Moguls and suggested that I might follow my own example in other chapters, who really prompted the chart repetition tactic.

To compile a chart seems a simple enough task: it would be infinitely simpler were it not for the penchant of Gresley, and indeed Thompson, to rebuild a stream of locomotives. What a nuisance they have been to me! When is an 'A1' an 'A10'? Which 'A1' is which in time? All one can do is to attempt to include each separate manifestation of the 4-6-2 wheel-arrangement. Inevitably, all the rebuilding leads to an apparently misleading total of Pacifics, if one looks only at the total of each class without noting the numbers of rebuilds. In fact, it is the small number in total of what is regarded in some quarters other than Swindon as the splendid zenith of the British express passenger steam locomotive, that may cause surprise.

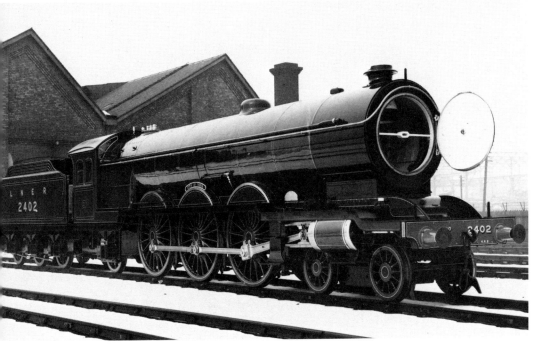

Left:
Surely as magnificent a sight as has ever graced a British railway: Raven Pacific No 2402 *City of York* **in LNER livery. Whatever these splendid engines may have lacked in performance relative to Gresley's designs, they surely would not be gainsaid in impressiveness of appearance. With memories of** *The Great Bear* **it is interesting to compare the modesty of the nameplate in contradistinction to Great Western practice. If only the preservation movement had come to maturity earlier.**

British Pacifics

Type	Number built	Driving wheel diameters	Date introduced	Railway	Designer	Builder/Works	Withdrawn	Notes
The Great Bear	1	6ft 8½in	1908	GWR	Churchward	Swindon	1924	First British Pacific
A1	2	6ft 2in	1922	GNR	Gresley	Doncaster	Rebuilt	Two original Gresley Pacifics: See 'A1' and 'A3' below. One, No 4470 *Great Northern* not rebuilt to 'A3', but to 'A1/1'
A2	5	6ft 8in	1922	NER	Raven	Darlington	1936/7	
A1	50	6ft 8in	1923	LNER	Gresley	Doncaster (30) NBL (20)	Rebuilt	Further orders by LNER, of GNR 'A1' as above, all except one rebuilt as Class A3
A3	78*	6ft 8in	1927	LNER	Gresley	Doncaster	Last 1966	*Total includes 51 rebuilt from Classes A1 and A10
'Princess Royal'	12	6ft 6in	1933	LMS	Stanier	Crewe	First 1961 / Last 1962	
Turbomotive	1	6ft 6in	1935	LMS	Stanier	Crewe	1954	Experimental version of 'Princess Royal' class, with turbine drive. Rebuilt 1952 as conventional locomotive.
A4	34	6ft 8in	1935	LNER	Gresley	Doncaster	First 1962 / Last 1966	
'Coronation'	38	6ft 6in	1937	LMS	Stanier	Crewe	First 1962 / Last 1964	24 were streamlined
'Merchant Navy'	30	6ft 2in	1941	SR	Bulleid	Eastleigh	First 1964 / Last 1967	All rebuilt, from 1956
A2/2	6	6ft 2in	1943	LNER	Thompson	Doncaster	First 1959 / Last 1961	Rebuilt from Gresley Class P2 2-8-2
A2/1	4	6ft 2in	1944	LNER	Thompson		1960/1	In effect, the final four 'V2' 2-6-2s, built as Pacifics
WC/BB Light Pacific	110	6ft 2in	1945	SR	Bulleid	Brighton*	First (un-rebuilt) 1963 / First (rebuilt) 1964 / Last 1967	*Six built at Eastleigh. The 'West Country' light Pacifics preceded the 'Battle of Britain', but were mechanically identical
A1/1	1	6ft 8in	1945	LNER	Thompson	Doncaster	1962	Controversial rebuild of Gresley's original 'Great Northern Pacific' (see above)
A2/3	15	6ft 2in	1946	LNER	Thompson	Doncaster	First 1962 / Last 1965	
A2	15	6ft 2in	1947	LNER	Peppercorn	Doncaster	First 1962 / Last 1966	
A1	49	6ft 8in	1948	LNER*	Peppercorn	Doncaster	First 1962 / Last 1966	*Peppercorn LNER design, entering service after the creation of BR in 1948
'Britannia' 7P 6F	55	6ft 2in	1951	BR	Riddles	Derby	First 1965 / Last 1968	
'Clan' 6P 5F	10	6ft 2in	1951	BR	Riddles	Derby	First 1962 / Last 1966	
8P	1	6ft 2in	1954	BR	Riddles	Derby	1962	*Duke of Gloucester*: saved for preservation

If one excepts *The Great Bear* and the Raven North Eastern Pacifics, and allows that the Gresley 'A1s' became his 'A3s', then it is possible to claim that every British Pacific class was still in active service into the final decade of steam on British Rail. This being so, space being limited, and 'new' material not being available, then this chapter will be more pictorial than literal, not least because the tales of the British Pacifics have been repeated and regurgitated so often. Each decade brought its own drama; how Gresley chose his own rather than Raven's locomotives for the LNER Pacifics; how the 'Castles' knocked spots off those same Gresley machines in the 1925 interchanges ('on any objective assessment the "Castle" outpointed the Pacific on almost every count, from coal consumption to timekeeping' — G. Freeman Allen, *Salute to the LNER*); the streamline battles between the LMS and LNER in the mid-1930s; Thompson's experiments and the outcry over *Great Northern* in the 1940s; the Bulleid era, and the brave deeds of steam's last great innovator, on the unlikely stage of the Southern; nationalisation, the efficient 'Britannias', and the rather forlorn 'Clans'; and then finally *Duke of Gloucester*. If *The Great Bear* was too early then the only BR '8P' Pacific was too late. Writing this, one is

reminded of the introductory music and words — should it be 'lyrics' — of the satirical television programme of the Macmillan era, *That Was The Week That Was*:

'It's all been done before
But so has spring and summer
We welcome them the more
For each is just a callow newcomer'

Glancing at the words written so far in this chapter, one name has yet to make its debut: Stanier. Surely his 'Coronation' Pacifics deserve a special mention. Dispassionately compared to their pre- and postwar contemporaries they seem to merit all-round acclaim. This is merely an impression based on nothing more than the opinion of the good and the great amongst those who have written about railway matters. It is purely subjective. Other Pacifics were perhaps more elegant, more mechanically exciting, more innovative, more publicity-attracting, although the Stanier engines had their fair share of all those attributes. Jane always admired the 'Coronations' and as a trained and qualified designer, her evaluation was as meritorious as mine, certainly. They actually lacked nothing in terms of appearance or mechanical ability. What more could one demand?

The rebirth of my railway enthusiasm coincided almost precisely with the demise of Stanier's first Pacifics, the 'Princess Royals', at the end of 1962. I never saw one, even on a scrap line. My predilection for 'things Great Western' will inevitably denude this chapter of GWR material save for mention of *The Great Bear*. Of Gresley's work my admiration for the 'A3' is not matched by enthusiasm for the 'A4'. The

Top:
For some, the Gresley 'A4' was, and is, the ultimate visual excitement. For me they did little when compared to an 'A3' or 'Coronation', to mention just Pacifics and to exclude Great Western locomotives. Here, one of these pregnant whales, No 60017 — obviously, *Silver Fox* — runs light engine alongside Peterborough New England Shed, on 7 July 1963. Removal of the valances and exposure of the 6ft 8in driving wheels certainly aided the appearance; but when dirty the streamlining emphasised the grime, and when immaculate they looked unreal.

Above:
On 18 May 1963, *Flying Scotsman* hauled the Gainsborough Model Railway Society special down to Eastleigh, where the Gresley Pacific was serviced. In her immaculate livery she looked out of place but outstanding amongst the rather grimy and dowdy Southern motive power that day a quarter of a century ago. A return visit would arouse great enthusiasm today amongst the Southern's steam-starved population.

aesthetic appeal of streamlining is quite lost on me. I like the sight of a good sturdy boiler, the all-round outline of a chimney. In this word-conscious age, dare I say that the 'A4' seemed 'effeminate'. Will this dread word be struck out by a sensitive editor? Will strictures flow from offended reviewers and readers? Streamlined skirts and cheeps of dainty whistles are the surrealist impression of the 'A4': whilst throaty roars of lusty masculinity recall the impression of a 'Duchess' on Shap. How incongruous — a masculine *Duchess of Hamilton* and an effeminate *William Whitelaw*! Surely not! Yet my ignorance of matters mechanical allows me only the choice of plagiarism, or concentration on appearances and surrealism if my words are to contain any originality. Which brings me to Bulleid.

Inevitably in considering the Pacifics of Bulleid one has to ask oneself the question — are you an 'unrebuilt' or a 'rebuilt' person? My comments on streamlining must presumably encompass 'air-smoothing', for Bulleid was disdainful of cosmetics for their own sake. The designer of the 'Q1' 0-6-0 would be, in all probability. Yet by 1963, the 'unrebuilts' were less common, and thus attracted attention for that very reason. If slang be vulgar, then in railway vernacular it was often attended by more than a hint of harsh veracity. He who coined the phrase 'Spam Can' may have been motivated by affectionate familiarity, or not; but the name stuck. Conversely, the unrebuilt Bulleids in their final form, Boxpok wheels clean and very visible, as epitomised by preserved 21C123 *Blackmore Vale* on the Bluebell Railway, is indeed a truly memorable and magnificent sight; and so is *Clan Line*, so one does not need to *choose* between the 'frocked' or 'unfrocked'. Perhaps after all it is the wheels themselves, the sight and visibility of which is an essential prerequisite to the visual appreciation of the steam engine.

The very first Pacific that I photographed was *Sun Castle* — an 'A2/3', one of the few classes that O. S. Nock does not even include in the comprehensive index of his *magnum opus British Locomotives of the 20th Century*. Alas poor Thompson, a much maligned man. 'Upheaval on the LNER' is the title with which Ossie Nock adorns his chapter on the taciturn man's era. Who could follow Gresley without seeming grey at best? Yet in those grim years of war and immediately thereafter, what chance did poor Thompson have? Could Collett indeed have outshone Churchward? Or Attlee, Churchill? Or Truman, Roosevelt? This is neither diversion nor digression, but merely postscripted thoughts upon the posthumous roles dictated by history to the characters therein. Of No 508, *Duke of Rothesay*, Ossie Nock captions the photograph with a reference to 'ungainly wheel spacing adopted for the Thompson Pacifics'; of No 4470 *Great Northern* he captions 'not an attractive locomotive . . .' Thus is the image of the man immortalised. Yet Brian Haresnape, taking a longer look at the Thompson locomotives in the perspective of their day, draws less harsh conclusions.

That photograph of *Sun Castle* was taken from the platform end at King's Cross in November 1962. Chronologically let me tabulate the first of each class of Pacific that appears in my catalogue.

Below:
My own camera was never aimed at one, but omission of a 'Princess Royal' class would have been inexcusable. On shed at Camden is No 46200 *The Princess Royal* in Maurice Earley's 1958 photograph.

Date	Class	CME	Number	Name	Location	Withdrawn	Scrapped
11.62	'A2/3'	Thompson	60523	*Sun Castle*	King's Cross	Jun 63	Doncaster Works August 63
2.63	'MN'	Bulleid	35005	*Canadian Pacific*	Queenstown Road Battersea	Oct 65	Preserved
2.63	'Rebuilt WC'*	Bulleid	34010	*Sidmouth*	Queenstown Road Battersea	Mar 65	Preserved
2.63	'A3'	Gresley	60071	*Tranquil*	Welwyn Garden City	Oct 64	Drapers, Hull January 65
2.63	'Coronation'	Stanier	46234	*Duchess of Abercorn*	Willesden	Jan 63	Crewe Works June 63
3.63	'A1'	Peppercorn	60117	*Bois Roussel*	Top Shed King's Cross	Jun 65	Clayton & Davis Dunston-on-Tyne October 65
3.63	'A4'	Gresley	60007	*Sir Nigel Gresley*	Top Shed King's Cross	Feb 66	Preserved
3.63	'Britannia'	Riddles	70021	*Morning Star*	Willesden	Dec 67	Wards, Inverkeithing Feb-May 68
5.63	'Unrebuilt BB'*	Bulleid	34061	*73 Squadron*	Basingstoke	Aug 64	Woods, Queenborough, Kent, March 65

*For the purpose of this chart the Bulleid Light Pacifics are treated as one class

Within the confines of time and my own working environment this list shows actually, even at this late hour of steam's active life, that I managed to fit in an example of most of those remaining active Pacifics within a very few weeks of starting my colour photography. For the purpose of simplicity I have not sought to 'extend' the list by adding, as an additional but separate entry, 'A3s' built as 'A1s' by the LNER and subsequently converted to 'A3', such as *Flying Scotsman* (LNER No 1472 then No 4472 then BR No 60103) nor by listing my first sightings of unrebuilt and rebuilt 'West Country' *and* 'Battle of Britain' classes. It also shows that, in spite of a lengthy vigil at Queenstown Road Battersea in February 1963 and visits to a number of Southern sheds it was not until mid-May 1963 that I saw an unrebuilt Bulleid Light Pacific. Perhaps of equal interest is the final chart, namely my last sightings of these classes of Pacifics, excluding sightings at Woodhams Barry, years later.

Left:
Modern journalism would no doubt cry 'obscene' to the act itself and to the end product of Thompson's rebuild of Gresley's pioneer Pacific. Brian Haresnape describes the dismantling and reconstruction of GNR No 1470/LNER No 4470/*Great Northern* as the 'most controversial of all the Thompson rebuilds', to produce what he calls 'a singularly ugly locomotive'. The layer of grime seen on 'A1/1' No 4470 at King's Cross in 1949, a year after rebuilding, helps to ameliorate, but can never cause to be forgiven, the feelings of anger which Gresley's unpopular successor brought upon his head by this infamous deed.

Above:
Of the Post-Grouping 'Big Four' the LNER was seemingly oblivious to the merits of standardisation as compared to the GWR and LMS: little continuity of policy was evident, with much tinkering around with rebuilding. After the trauma of Thompson, A. H. Peppercorn had but two years on which to leave his stamp, and his 6ft 8in Pacifics themselves were based on Thompson's Class A1/1 No 60113, itself the rebuild of Gresley's original Pacific No 4470 *Great Northern*. None of the 49 Peppercorn 'A1' class survived into preservation: my sightings were absolutely minimal. Here, No 60146 *Peregrine* stands outside Top Shed at King's Cross in March 1963. Alongside is '9F' 2-10-0 No 92145.

Below:
Bulleid 'Battle of Britain' class 4-6-2 No 34061 *73 Squadron* stands beside the coal stage at Basingstoke MPD on 18 May 1963, a much less common sight, of course, especially clean, than the rebuilt engines with air-smoothed casing removed.

Left:

Rebuilt 'Battle of Britain' 4-6-2 No 34056 *Croydon*, having coaled, awaits her turn on the 'table' at Nine Elms on 7 July 1964. The driver enjoys his chance of immortality through the lens of my trusty Voigtlander, which seemed to take better pictures than my new-fangled Canon A1, which is too clever for me. There are still three years to go before the end of steam at Nine Elms, by which time No 34056 will have failed by two months to be one of the final Southern steam survivors; she was withdrawn from Salisbury shed in May 1967.

Above:

With less than four months to go before the end of Southern steam, the last Bulleid 'Merchant Navy' No 35030 *Elder Dempster Lines* heads west past Nine Elms on 23 March 1967. The headcode indicates a West of England line express. In those last few months from Waterloo, on what ironically became London's last main line steam passenger service, drivers and firemen struggled with often ill-maintained steeds to ensure that steam went out not with a whimper but with a bang. The gasometer is just one more landmark that has disappeared hereabouts. The first 20 'Merchant Navys' were built by the SR: the last 10 completed by BR. Early in 1956, No 35018 was completely rebuilt and the streamlining removed, all 30 being so treated by the end of 1959.

shape of No 35028 *Clan Line* would bring Bulleid glory back to London, turn and turn about with an 'A4' and a 'Coronation'?

At the start of this chapter I confessed my difficulty in finding anything new or original to say about Pacifics. My personal recollections have had to suffice. If apologies are due, they are offered. 'From *The Great Bear* to *Duke of Gloucester*' spans the mortal being of the British Pacific — immortalised perhaps above all others by the late Eric Treacy. He, like the spirit of Churchward, of Gresley, of Stanier, of Bulleid, and of the unsung design office and workshop heroes without the glamour of the great names, has woven his spell over us lesser mortals. As Magnus Magnusson would say 'I've started, so I'll finish'. There indeed were the Masterminds of steam. We thank them, we praise them, we salute them all.

Top:

Bulleid 'West Country' Pacific No 34038 *Lynton* rests inside Bristol St Philips Marsh roundhouse, on 26 January 1963. These unrebuilt engines looked particularly forlorn when dirty. I had just started my railway photography, was not researching my subject so have no notes about the working by which this Eastleigh engine arrived at St Philips Marsh, which was soon to close. Presumably she had worked into Bristol from the Salisbury direction, on a Portsmouth-Bristol train.
Author

CHAPTER EIGHT

MOGUL

'It struck me that there was an opening for such a mixed-traffic engine on British Railways.'

Harold Holcroft

At first sight, Pigs and Crabs would appear to have little in common, and certain it is that neither creature summons instantly to mind an image to fit the Oxford dictionary's definition of 'Mogul'. Perhaps before embarking on my dissertation on the British 2-6-0, we should spend a moment seeking the origins of the word 'Mogul' to describe this wheel-arrangement.

It is generally assumed that the descriptive adjectives used to denote various wheel-arrangements emanate from the United States, whence Pacific, Atlantic, Prairie, Consolidation, as well as Mogul, may be traced or attributed. Baltic clearly does not fit into this pattern; but it is not my purpose here to pontificate on nomenclature. Suffice it to say that the first British 2-6-0, No 527 of the Great Eastern Railway, reputedly had the name *Mogul* inscribed on the large sandbox above the middle driving wheels. Contemporaneous with public interest in the Great Mogul of Delhi, some railway historians claim No 527 as the progenitor of the title 'Mogul' for the 2-6-0. Other evidence points across the Atlantic, where it was, and remains, a national characteristic to identify size with power and influence, notwithstanding Vietnam. Whatever the genuine origins of the word in locomotive parlance, however, there can be no doubting the clear American antecedence in the development of the 2-6-0.

American experience was undoubtedly utilised in those GER machines. Whilst we today use the phrase 'mixed traffic' as a matter of course, in the early railway years locomotives tended either to be goods or passenger machines. Bearing in mind the industrial origins of railways, the speed of techno-logical development of the locomotive, and the

genealogy of the phrase 'built-in obsolescence' one can find it understandable that these factors combined into two features of American railway practice, namely a willingness to experiment boldly with new wheel-arrangements; and the belief that the speed of technological change itself militated against any intention to design locomotives — particularly freight engines — for long life. Thus those Great Eastern 2-6-0s and their successors, US-built engines for the Great Northern, the Great Central and the Midland Railways, owed much to Transatlantic practice.

Neilson built the first GER 2-6-0 in 1878, and the wheels themselves were of interest. The leading pony truck was very similar to that contempor-aneously in use on the Pennsylvania Rail Road; whilst the original driving-wheels on the centre axle were built without tyres. Later, however, they were replaced by flanged tyres. Other 'un-British' features characterised these Massey Bromley locomotives, which were originally designed by one of the great names of the British railway scene, namely William Adams, Locomotive Superintendent of the Great Eastern from 1873-1878, immediately prior to his arrival at Nine Elms, where his work as Mechanical Engineer of the LSWR is undoubtedly better known. Lest I digress, however, Adams' work on the GER Moguls was modified by his successor Massey Bromley, whose 3-year reign at Stratford in charge of matters mechanical on the 'Swedie' included the period of the introduction of Britain's first 2-6-0. At the time of writing these words, based on information gleaned from various sources including *The LNER 2-6-0 Class* by Messrs Clay and Cliffe, I cannot recall seeing many photographs or indeed much comment on these locomotives other than in their book.

Sadly, Adams and Bromley appear not to have produced a great locomotive, perhaps in itself the reason for the paucity of information. Predating the

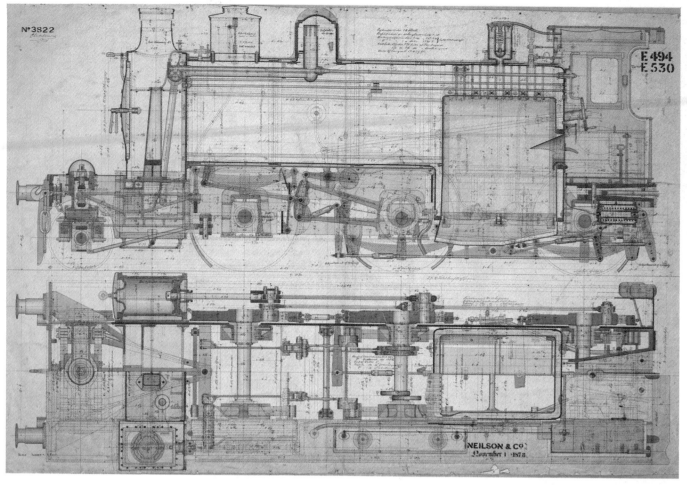

Nº 3822

E 494
E 530

NEILSON & Cº
November 1 1878

Above:

As this drawing is dated 1 December 1878 it must be assumed that Neilson's customer was an overseas railway — see chart of British Moguls on page 134.

'mixed-traffic' era, the Neilson-built engine's performance centred on sluggish running, poor steaming and heavy fuel-consumption. With the Great Eastern's reputation for doing things on the cheap, it is possible that the company that ordered them, rather than the company that built them, was the root cause of the problem. Whatever the rights and wrongs of the matter, all 15 were scrapped between 1885-87; and the resulting gap in further construction of British 2-6-0s coincided with a reversion, by the GER, to the 'safer' and more traditional 0-6-0 for their freight work. Nearly 20 years elapsed before another 2-6-0 appeared on British metals; and these were yet another oddity. In 1895, one small Mogul, built by Beyer Peacock for a South American customer, never reached its destination for commercial reasons and was purchased from the builders by the Midland & South Western Junction Railway (MSWJ). It was so well thought-of that another was ordered by the MSWJ two years later and will always be remembered for her delightful nickname, 'Galloping Alice'. No more Moguls were built in Britain until the 20th century; but that is by no means the end of the 'American Connection'.

At the turn of the century Britain's railways were booming, and many were experiencing difficulty in obtaining sufficient locomotives for their increasing needs. Rixon Bucknall in *Our Railway History* affords but two sentences in a chapter on The Midland, to explain that railway's situation. 'In 1899 some 2-6-0 goods locomotives were ordered from America to meet an urgent demand which could not be supplied by this country. Judged by British standards these engines were not an economical proposition on the score of running costs and maintenance, and their lives, in consequence, were short.' In fact, the Midland ordered 40 of these Moguls; 30 from Baldwins and 10 from the Schenectady Works. Whilst the former, with their twin domes and bogie tenders, appeared typically American, the latter were of much more British appearance, with small splashers and Midland Railway six-wheel tenders. It was performance rather than appearance that accounted for their achievement of an unenviable record — the shortest life of any working Midland Railway class. By 1915, the last of the 'Yankees' had been scrapped.

The Great Northern and the Great Central 2-6-0s, to which I referred briefly earlier, were also built at the Baldwin Locomotive Works in Philadelphia. Smaller than the Neilson Great Eastern Moguls, the GN and GC each ordered 20 engines. Both railways assembled these locomotives in their own works, the former at Ardsley and the latter at Gorton, where

Above:
LMS Ivatt taper boiler '4MT' 2-6-0 No 43041 passes Plumley
West Box, on the former Cheshire Lines Committee (CLC)
line between Altrincham and Northwich, with the 17.38
Manchester Central-Cuddington train, in April 1964. Known
as 'Flying Pigs', with 5ft 3in wheels, the first 50 locomotives
built (three by the LMS prior to nationalisation) were fitted
with double blastpipes and chimneys but, owing to poor
steaming, these were later replaced with a more satisfactory
single version.Notice the delightful signal, and the driver, who
probably saw few photographers on this line. The BR-built
engines were completed between 1948 and 1952, following
numerically straight on from the original LMS trio.

Below:
Neither rust, neglect nor impending destruction can destroy
the classic lines of Churchward's '43xx' class. Introduced in
1911, their light axle-loading gave them an extensive route
availability which, added to versatility, would see them on
almost any duty, from Cambrian lines to Reading-Redhill
passenger duty, and freight service almost anywhere on Great
Western metals. No 6391 ended her days as a Reading (81D)
engine, whence she was withdrawn in September 1962, and
where I photographed her on 4 May 1963. Behind her, on the
scrap road, is No 4921 *Eaton Hall*, also a Reading engine,
withdrawn also the previous September. *Valete*

Below:
Few uglier machines ever emerged from Swindon than the '2601' class, known without affection as the 'Krugers'. Ten were built, the last being No 2610 seen here. Really a bastard sired at the end of the Dean era, but before Churchward assumed full control, these large double-framed engines portrayed the latter's influence in its domeless Belpaire boiler. They were as unsuccessful as they were unlovely, but their boilers survived at Swindon for another 60 years in stationary use.

Bottom:
The Great Western 'Aberdare' class 2-6-0 was a remarkable locomotive, being the first six-coupled engine to carry the type of boiler that, almost 50 years later, became the accepted form on the BR Standard classes. Visually, however, the double frames — a feature of Victorian rather than Elizabethan design — distinguished the 'Aberdares'. Attributed to Dean, but really a product of Churchward, the 'Aberdare' or '2621' class went into quantity production in 1901. Here No 2669 enters Stapleton Road station, Bristol, with a 'J' class stopping mixed freight. Stapleton Road was in my old constituency of Bristol North-East, but sadly by 1970 the 'Aberdares' were but a memory . . .

most of them were stationed. One can only wonder at the comments of the GN men when they first saw these machines. They could hardly have been more different from the succession of elegant locomotives which H. A. Ivatt was designing and building at Doncaster. Perhaps they would have been more appropriate under the *imprimatur* of his latter-day kinsman H. G. Ivatt, whose unlovely Class 4MT creation earned that memorable 'Flying Pig' tag; by a strange quirk of history also a 2-6-0. It too owed much in its day (1947) to contemporary American practice, with its emphasis on exposed parts for ease of servicing; but the 'Flying Pigs' came later in the history of the Mogul. Much water was to flow under the bridge between 1899 and 1947.

The Great Northern's American-built Moguls spent much of their working lives on coal trains in the Leeds area, and later in the Nottinghamshire coalfield. Photographs of the GNR Baldwins are not common, yet in that railway's livery they looked quite smart, rather than in any way elegant. Occasionally these essentially freight engines worked

Above:
A Churchward Mogul in her prime: '43xx' 2-6-0 No 4331 heads a down excursion to Stonehenge, past Sonning Box in 1928. One can but imagine what the master photographers of 60 years ago would have created with fast colour film.

the odd secondary passenger service, and some finished their days allocated to Hornsea Shed. Scrapping commenced in 1911. So, as with the Midland engines, these American locomotives did not last long.

Of the Great Central's 'Yankees' there is little to say. They too were essentially freight engines. Those not based at Gorton were allocated when new to Lincoln and New Holland, whilst later some went to Leicester, where their booked tasks included workings to Ardsley. I do not know if they met up there with their Great Northern cousins. Whilst based at Leicester they occasionally worked holiday excursion trains to East Coast resorts, as well as handling local passenger services to Nottingham, Rugby and Woodford Halse. They were graded Class 4 on the GCR power classification scheme.

Whilst the GCR, GNR and Midland's American 2-6-0s were not significant in themselves, they bridge a gap in the 2-6-0 story. High on running and maintenance costs and low on quality and longevity, they nevertheless illustrated the development of Transatlantic practice, and indeed in their cheapness the philosophy of built-in obsolescence to which I have referred. The gap they helped to bridge was really the gap between 19th and 20th centuries: between Ivatt and Dean before Gresley and Churchward. Indeed it was one of the latter's brightest young men at Swindon, Harold Holcroft, who persuaded the great man to listen to him following a visit he made to America. Holcroft was convinced that a Swindon 2-6-0 with larger driving wheels would fill a gap in GWR motive power requirements; a speedier machine than the Dean Goods, able to work passenger and freight trains with equal efficiency. Thus the first of the new generation of British Moguls were born, at Swindon,

in 1911. Before we examine the '43xx' class, however, there is another span to that gap: for it was not just Holcroft's American experience that fathered the GWR's '43xx' Moguls. Of undoubted relevance to this development were the 'Aberdares', themselves an evolution of Great Western practice insofar as tapered boilers were concerned. The tapered boiler can be recognised, even by someone like myself with no engineering knowledge, as one of the most significant developments in steam locomotive anthropology. It was the success of the 'Camel' and 'Atbara' classes that was applied to the 2-6-0 wheel arrangement for the first time that enables me to claim that the 'Aberdare' class was the machine that spanned the gap, insofar as the 2-6-0 is concerned, between 19th and 20th century practice.

The 'Aberdare' class gained their name from the nature of their main usage on the heavy South Wales coal trains from Aberdare to Swindon, notwithstanding the fact that, when first introduced, they were running in gorgeous GWR style, with gleaming brass and copper, magnificent paintwork and much lining-out. What a sight they must have been — oh for colour film at the turn of the century! The first Great Western 2-6-0, No 33 (renumbered 2600 in 1912), had 4ft 7½in wheels with outside bearings, a two-wheeled inside-framed leading truck, and 18in×26in cylinders. Design work began in 1899; completed in August 1900, to William Dean's design, it became the prototype 'Aberdare'.

Top left:
With my photography commencing at the end of 1962, it coincided with the mass withdrawal of the entire class of the 17 Billinton 'K' class. Introduced in 1913, they survived intact until November/December 1962. No 32341, a longtime Brighton (75A) engine, languishes here on the scrap line at Hove, on 17 February 1963. Another 'K' is behind No 32341, and she faces yet another Mogul, as is self-evident. The 'Ks' were the only non-Maunsell Moguls on Southern Region to survive into the 1960s.

Left:
The stark lines and high running-plate of the Ivatt LMS '4MT' Moguls are self-evident here. On 14 May 1964 Watford's (1C) own No 43021 illustrates the reason why the class earned the ugly tag of 'Flying Pig'. The Mogul on Britain's railways, with its early American influence, came full circle with the LMS-inspired BR 2-6-0s with their transatlantic emphasis on function rather than charm. One can only be grateful for the works of Gresley in between.

Above:
Churchward '43xx' 2-6-0 No 6346 rests under the roundhouse roof of St Philips Marsh MPD, Bristol, on 23 January 1963. Note the smoke-extractors located fore and aft of each arm of the turntable, to cater for locomotives moving forwards or in reverse from the turntable to rest. *Author*

No 33 was a product of the Dean-Churchward interregnum, to which reference is made by John Booth in his introduction to issue No 45 of *Locomotives Illustrated*. He sums up this pregnant period of GWR locomotive evolution thus:

'But what is curious is the appearance of some very odd designs, or combinations of old and new, in the short transitional period before the multiplication of the Churchward standard types. One wonders on whose authority some of the more outlandish designs appeared — do they represent the last outworkings of Dean's mind or the first, as yet unsuccessful, essays on the part of Churchward?'

The greatest oddity within this outlandish story concerns locomotive No 2601: it was a 2-6-0 with a 4-6-0 wheel-arrangement! As a cackhanded way of explaining the situation, let me quote from MacDermott's *History of the Great Western Railway*, in which he describes No 2602 as 'being practically identical with 2601, except for having its front end supported on a two-wheeled truck like 33'. 2601 always ran as a 4-6-0, but is listed as one of the 10 'Krugers': surely an unique example of one single class having one member thereof with a different wheel-arrangement.

No 2602 was apparently designed as a 4-6-0, and was indeed very similar to the experimental No 2601; but it eventually emerged as a 2-6-0. Coinciding with the Boer War, this odd, ugly machine and its mates, Nos 2603-10, were nicknamed 'Krugers'. This was not, nor was it intended to be complimentary. Time has eroded both memory and detailed reasoning as to the construction of these further 'Krugers', *after*

Searching for information and photographs of the Baldwin and Schenectady 2-6-0s supplied to the Midland, Great Northern and Great Central Railways at the turn of the century has led me far beyond the NRM Library. Having contacted the Smithsonian Institution in Washington, they put me in contact with Herb Broadbelt of Newport News, Virginia, who had purchased the Baldwin Locomotive Works photographic negatives. Compare the official Baldwin photograph of Midland Railway No 2501 (*left*) with No 2526 (*below*) at Lancaster MPD sometime between 1903-06. Such information as has emerged led me to believe that the Baldwin engines had double domes (in fact the second 'dome' was a sandbox), whilst the Schenectady batch had a more 'British' look. However, GNR No 1200 (*next page, top*) from Herb Broadbelt's Baldwin negatives has not only clean lines, but an 'Ivatt' chimney. The last of this quartet of photographs features MR No 2516 (*bottom*), with distinctive differences including six-wheel tender. The works plate denotes Schenectady Locomotive Works.

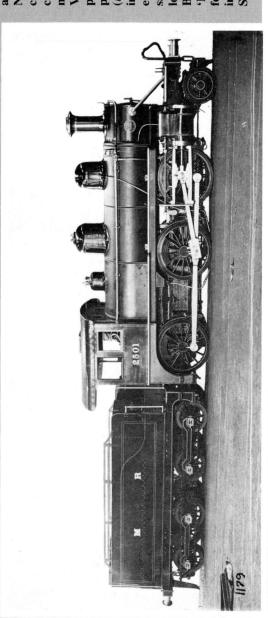

the appearance of the more conventional 2-6-0 No 33, which became the prototype 'Aberdare' class.

Eventually 81 'Aberdares' were built by December 1902. Unlike their Baldwin contemporaries, these Swindon machines survived for about half a century, the last 'Aberdare', No 2620, being withdrawn in August 1949 after the creation of British Railways. Indeed, on the last day of the independent existence of the GWR, 31 December 1947, 12 'Aberdares' were still 'on the books' as part of that railway's current stock: there were, by then, 241 Moguls of the Churchward '43xx' class and its successors, too.

If reading these last few paragraphs has caused as much confusion to you as it has to my long-suffering secretary Kay Dixon, then I can only apologise, and turn with relief from the awful 'Krugers', and the ancient 'Aberdares', to the Churchward '43xx' Moguls. Here we arrive at the father of the modern British Mogul, and the first in this chapter which enables me to include one of my own colour photographs. Much has been written about these outstanding locomotives. The first was built in 1911: construction continued, with comparatively minor modifications, by Churchward's successor, Collett, whose version of the GWR Standard Mogul came out in 1932. As this book is called *Wheels* it is relevant to mention one modification; the '43xx' class engines working in the West Country suffered excessive flange wear, due to the sharp track curvature, particularly in Devon, and Cornwall where they operated virtually the entire passenger and freight service in the early 1920s. Consequently, 65 members of the class were modified — as had been four of the earlier engines — in 1928 by moving the buffer beam forward and placing a large casting behind, in order to bring extra weight on to the pony truck. This modification was removed from the Collett engines in 1956, due to the shortage caused by withdrawals by this date of locomotives with a lower axle loading.

The '43xx' was a total synthesis of standard parts, using the outside cylinders of the 'Saint', the wheels of the '31xx' 2-6-2T, and the No 4 boiler in its superheated form. Although withdrawals of the early Churchward engines began in 1936, it was not for scrapping but for conversion and use of the components for the 'Manor' and 'Grange' 4-6-0s. By this time numbering 342 in all, it is said that all the

Moguls would in due course have been so converted. However, the war intervened and prevented this happening. My sightings were infrequent, but included one of my few black-and-white photographs, of 1923-built No 6346, which survived until June 1964. They handled heavy goods trains easily as well as an 'Aberdare', whilst eminently capable of 70mph running on passenger trains. It was the demise of steam, not of their usefulness, which brought extinction.

Lest anyone should dispute the claim that George Jackson Churchward was the father of the modern British steam locomotive, let it be recalled that one of the final batch of 'Aberdare' class engines became the first six-coupled engine to carry the taper boiler. This feature epitomised the Standard classes of the nationalised British Railways nearly half a century later, not to mention the works of Churchward's Swindon-trained disciple, one William Stanier.

After this confusion, it might be appropriate now to tabulate the evolution of the British 2-6-0. My choice of this moment, namely after Churchward's Mogul, but before Gresley's, emphasises my belief that it was industrial espionage rather than mere coincidence that resulted in the emergence in 1912 of Gresley's Great Northern 2-6-0. These fine engines gave birth to a family of GNR and LNER Moguls, adopted by Gresley as the LNER standard mixed-traffic type, very many of which lasted into the final decade of steam. There are, however, two other small classes of British 2-6-0 which post-dated the original Gresley engines but which did not, by virtue of heritage and small numbers rather than design or performance, survive so long. These were five Caledonian engines built in 1912 and Peter Drummond's 11 handsome express goods locomotives on the Glasgow & South Western Railway (G&SW). The Caledonian inside-cylinder 2-6-0s were literally an elongated main line version of the 0-6-0s used by that railway on the Clyde coast trains. They were the first Moguls to run in Scotland, and in their day spearheaded the main line freight workings on the Caley main line between Glasgow and Carlisle. They were, however, not really in quite the same class as Peter Drummond's G&SW Moguls — an outstanding locomotive from a distinguished member of a great railway family.

A beautiful colour illustration of the Drummond engine by Clifford and Wendy Meadway is featured in O. S. Nock's *Pocket Encyclopaedia of British Steam Locomotives* and causes one to gnash one's teeth in frustration at never having seen such a splendid machine. Introduced on the G&SW in 1915, they too were an answer to the traffic department's call for a goods engine suitable to 20th century needs. Superheated, and much heavier than the previous 0-6-0 goods engines at work on the steeply-graded main lines, the pony-truck insertion created a locomotive of a very different calibre — namely a modern superheated 2-6-0 rather than a

Left:
Designed at Derby and introduced in 1953, the BR Standard Class 2MT Moguls were, with their larger Class 4MT fellows, the last of the British 2-6-0s. They were very similar to the LMS Ivatt Moguls, both having 5ft wheels. No 78035 makes good use of her ejectors — not unhelpfully for my camera — on Watford shed, on 14 May 1964.

The 2-6-0 on Britain's Railways
(Outside cylinders unless noted)

Type	Number built	Driving wheel diameter	Date introduced	Railway	Designer	Builder/ Works	Traffic utilisation	Withdrawn	Notes
'Mogul'	15	4ft 10in	1878/9	GER	Massey Bromley	Neilson	Goods	1885-87	First British 2-6-0
Nos 14 and 16	2	4ft 0in	1895	MSWJR		Beyer Peacock (orig for South America)	Goods	1914*/1930	'Galloping Alice' (16) *Sold for colliery use and finally scrapped in 1943
'Yankees'	30 10 20 20	5ft 0in 5ft 0in 5ft 1½in ?	1899 1899/ 1900	Midland GNR GCR	Burnham & Williams	Baldwin Schenectady Baldwin	Goods Goods	1911-1915	Not considered to have made any material contribution to British locomotive practice or development
'Kruger'	10	4ft 7½in	1899	GWR	Dean/ Churchward	Swindon	Goods	Last one 1906	Inside cylinders and inside framed bogie. No 2601, the prototype, ran as a 4-6-0 throughout its life. (See text)
'Aberdare'	81	4ft 7½in	1901	GWR	Dean/ Churchward	Swindon	Goods	1936-49	Prototype No 33 was generically similar to 'Atbara' class 4-4-0
43xx	342	5ft 8in	1911	GWR	Churchward	Swindon	Mixed traffic	1936-64	Total includes later Collett derivatives of original Churchward locomotives. Early withdrawals were rebuilt to 4-6-0
34	5	5ft 0in	1912	Caledonian	McIntosh	St Rollox	Fast goods	Mid-thirties	Modification of '30' class 0-6-0; engines virtually identical save for longer frame and pony-truck. Inside cylinders
H2 (K1)	10	5ft 8in	1912	GNR	Gresley	Doncaster	Fast goods	1937	Gresley's first Mogul
K	17	5ft 6in	1913	LBSCR	Billinton	Brighton	Express goods	1962	Built from 1913 to 1921: the first class of Mogul that I photographed
H3 (K2) 'Ragtimer'	75	5ft 8in	1914	GNR	Gresley	Doncaster NBL Kitson	Mixed traffic	1955 First 1962 Last	'Ragtimer' nickname due to rough-riding. 75 includes 10 H2 rebuilds
Drummond Superheater	11	5ft 0in	1915	Glasgow & South Western	Peter Drummond	Kilmarnock	Express goods	Last three: mid-forties	Inside cylinders
N	80	5ft 6in	1917	SECR & SR	Maunsell	Ashford Woolwich	Mixed traffic	1962-66	Prototype built by Maunsell for SECR; building continued until 1934. 50 were built at Woolwich Arsenal.
H4 (K3)	193	5ft 8in	1920	GNR	Gresley	Doncaster	Mixed trafic	1959 First 1962 Last	3-cylinder locomotives: nicknamed 'Jazzers'. No 206 rebuilt as 2-cylinder 'K5' in 1945
N1	6	5ft 6in	1923	SECR & SR	Maunsell	Ashford	Mainly passenger	1962	3-cylinder engines; prototype by Maunsell for SECR: remaining five built 1930
U	20+30	6ft 0in	1925	SR	Maunsell	Brighton Ashford Eastleigh	Mixed traffic	1962-66	20 originally built as 2-6-4T 'River' class in 1917 by SECR remainder built new as 2-6-0
Crab	245	5ft 6in	1926	LMS	Hughes-Fowler	Horwich Crewe	Mixed traffic	1961-67	Based on a Caledonian design of 2-6-0 that was never actually built. Basically designed for freight working, but versatility earned mixed-traffic rating
U1	21	6ft 0in	1928	SR	Maunsell	Ashford Eastleigh	Mainly passenger	1962-63	3-cylinder engines: first was built as 2-6-4T 'River' class (see above); remainder built new as 2-6-0 in 1931
5F (Later varied)	40	5ft 6in	1933	LMS	Stanier	Crewe	Mainly goods	1963-67	Stanier's first new design for LMS; strong Great Western features
K4	6	5ft 2in	1937	LNER	Gresley	Darlington	Mixed traffic	1961 last	3-cylinder engines for West Highland line
K1/1	1	5ft 2in	1945	LNER	Thompson	Darlington	Mixed traffic	1961	Rebuild of 'K4': 2 cylinders
K5	1	5ft 8in	1945	LNER	Thompson	Darlington	Mixed traffic	1960	No 1863 rebuilt from K3, with 2 cylinders (see above)
2P/2F	128	5ft 0in	1946	20×LMS 108×BR	H. G. Ivatt	LMS Crewe BR Crewe, Darlington, Swindon	Light duty mixed traffic	1961-67	First really modern small steam engines produced in Britain for many years
4P/4F	162	5ft 2in	1947	3×LMS 159×BR	H. G. Ivatt	LMS Horwich BR Horwich, Doncaster, Darlington	Mixed traffic	1963-68	'Flying Pig': design features similar to contemporary American practice
K1	70	5ft 2in	1949	LNER	Peppercorn	NBL	Mixed traffic	1967 Last	Peppercorn development of Thompson 'K1/1'
BR2 78000	65	5ft 0in	1952	BR	Riddles	Derby	Mixed traffic	1963-67	Modified version of Ivatt LMS 2P/2F as above†
BR4 76000	115	5ft 3in	1952	BR	Riddles	Doncaster	Mixed traffic	1963-67	Modified version of Ivatt LMS 4P/4F as above†
BR3 77000	20	5ft 3in	1954	BR	Riddles	Swindon	Light passenger	1965-67	Too late on scene; replaced by diesel railcars almost as soon as built†

Footnote: †For charting convenience, all three BR locomotives are attributed to R. A. Riddles

Victorian traditional 0-6-0. David Smith, doyen of writers about the G&SW, records one running at 70mph through Kilkerran. All five Caledonian Moguls had gone by the mid-1930s, but three of the G&SW batch lasted into the war years, seeing service on the far north road of the Highland Railway. The Caledonian and G&SW machines were quite distinctively different.

The accompanying chart is inserted here in this chapter because we now reach not only the mainstream of modern Mogul development, but also the point at which I am able to supplement historic cribbing with personal recollection, although this unfortunately does not apply to any of the GNR/LNER/BR Eastern Region Moguls. My lack of personal sightings of any of these — the 'H2s', 'H3s' and 'H4s' of the GNR (then reclassified as 'K1s', 'K2s' and 'K3s' of the LNER); plus 'K4', then 'K1/1', 'K5' and 'K1' — justifies my skating quickly over a series of Moguls which played a major part in the work of the GNR and LNER. Essentially the work of Sir Nigel Gresley, they fell prey to the attentions of Edward Thompson, whose 'K1/1' was a rebuild of the 'K4'; whilst the 'K1' of 1949 was Peppercorn's development of Thompson's 'K1/1'. These latter 'K1s', classified 5P6F, were the final flowering of the Mogul prior to the British Rail Standard designs.

Enough confusion, for me certainly, surrounds the attempt to chart the Gresley/Thompson/Peppercorn

Mogul manifestation. What, obviously, is not in any way mentioned, let alone charted in a chapter included in a book such as this, are the numerous locomotives that were not built. These range from the enhanced doodles by enthusiastic and aspiring junior members of the railway workshop design teams, up through the more advanced proposals from the design offices. E. S. Cox in *Locomotive Panorama* recalls the birth of the 'Crab', and the work done on a 'large mixed traffic 2-6-0 worked out in some detail at St Rollox. This engine, which carried features common with the Caledonian "60" and ex-Highland "River" classes, had large horizontal outside cylinders which ruled it out at once for use on any of the English lines. A fresh start was therefore made at Horwich and many versions were offered before the design was finally frozen for production'. We shall come to the 'Crab' in a moment.

When one comes to write chapters such as this, it is inevitable that much information is derived from

snippets gleaned from the labours of numerous authors. Such reading gives one an insight into the characters of the actors on the stage of steam. One learns that behind the heroes, the giants, the men like Churchward, Gresley, Stanier, *et al*, there stood the lesser-known men, whose names are of course household words to, shall we say, members of the Institution of Mechanical Engineers, but less well-known to the occasional readers of railway books. One thinks of men like Roland Bond or, from an earlier era, Harold Holcroft, who served their apprenticeship under one great man and whose careers 'failed' only in that they never received a knighthood or public acclamation. Yet their contribution to railway engineering developments was immense, and now in retrospect they are being recognised, written about and appreciated for their true worth. Gresley indeed behaved rather badly towards Holcroft in that he 'stole' the latter's derived conjugated valve gear and claimed it as his own. From Swindon, Holcroft himself was enticed by Richard Maunsell to Ashford in 1913, when the latter became CME of the South Eastern & Chatham.

Having, therefore, looked at the Great Western and Gresley Moguls, as well as the small numbers of Caledonian, G&SW and 19th century 2-6-0s, let us turn to the constituents of the Southern, namely the LBSCR and SECR Moguls, still around in the 1960s.

LBSC 'Ks' Nos 32338 and 32341/2 and Maunsell three-cylinder 'U1' No 31891 were the first Moguls that I photographed. Sadly they were all on a line of dumped and withdrawn engines at Hove on 17 February 1963, although the 'U1' was not officially withdrawn until April that year. The 17 Billinton 'Ks' were all withdrawn in November and December 1962, at the precise time of my first tentative colour photography. Of those three that I saw at Hove, No 32338 (one of the original 1913 locomotives) had run 1,081,627 miles in its 49-year life from December 1913 to December 1962.

Billinton's Moguls were both rugged and handsome. Built with Robinson superheaters, large outside cylinders, Stephenson valve gear and a Belpaire firebox, the first five emerged from Brighton Works at a cost of £3,150 each. To mention such a figure today, when a secondhand Ford Fiesta costs about the same, is perhaps totally meaningless; yet I was able to see and photograph a number of the

Left:
Steam, freight, colour-light and semaphore signals, and colour too; the steam scene epitomised by one of my favourite classes, the Hughes-Fowler 'Crab'. Transferred to Stockport some six months previously, No 42734, with safety valves lifting, restarts her train, hemmed in by Newton Heath coal stage on the left and the carriage works, bathed in winter sunshine, on the right. The date is 3 December 1964. Fine engines, those 'Crabs'.

137

class — after withdrawal but before scrapping. How very sad it is that none survived. If only one or two has found their way to Dai Woodham's scrapyard we might be able still to enjoy their lines.

Although designed and built primarily for the express goods trains of the LBSCR, especially the Continental services to and from Newhaven, they could cope well with 1,000-ton trains on the main lines. They proved invaluable during World War 1 on troop specials bound for Newhaven. Freight, however, remained their task throughout their existence, which accounts for the comparative disinterest they engendered until the twilight of their lives. Unlike some of the Ashford 'Ns' and 'Us', none of the 'Ks' needed either new frames or cylinders during their lifetime, and their withdrawal was 'political' in line with the phasing-out of steam. Thus is the waste of good resources only too well illustrated. The Billinton 'Ks' may not, in themselves, have played a distinctive role in the evolution and history of the British Mogul, but they were excellent engines. We miss them.

If the 'K' was in itself a mundane and unexciting locomotive, then no such modest attribute attended the introduction of SECR No 810, in August 1917. Maunsell's first Mogul was considered to be one of the finest and most advanced locomotives yet built. It was the first of a long line of distinctive designs, firstly for the South Eastern & Chatham and, after the 1923 Grouping, for the Southern Railway. The main factor linking Billinton's 'K' and Maunsell's 'N', was the common requirement of the traffic departments of both the LBSCR and SECR for a modern locomotive capable of handling heavy freight trains at reasonable speed on busy main lines; and certainly as far as the 'N' was concerned, an engine able to cope with all but the heaviest and fastest passenger duties.

Having already written a chapter about the Maunsell Moguls — 'SECR and the Maunsell Moguls' — in an earlier book, it is not my intention to repeat what has already been written. In terms of the Mogul story though, Maunsell's arrival at Ashford, and his immediate 'poaching' of two of Swindon's brightest young engineers, G. H. Pearson and Harold Holcroft — as already mentioned — inevitably influenced his first new design. It was, after all, only six years after the introduction of Churchward's '43xx' class. A glance at the chart on page 134 shows only the driving-wheel sizes, as it is not intended remotely to be a source of technical information. That these wheels were within 2in of each other in size is but one similarity between the two designs. Indeed, with its taper boiler, top feed, working pressure and long-lap valves, the 'N' had a distinctly Swindon flavour, and was none the worse for that. Other features were much more in the Derby mould, for in addition to Pearson and Holcroft from Swindon, Maunsell had persuaded James Clayton from the Midland HQ to join him at

Ashford. Thus the 'N' had incorporated within it the best practices from two of the country's most prominent locomotive works. O. S. Nock has described No 810 with the companion 2-6-4T No 790, as 'the most outstanding locomotive built for service in this country since the pioneer work of Churchward in 1903-7'.

The story of the 'Woolworths' from Woolwich Arsenal, which formed the bulk of the production runs of the 'Ns' for the Southern, has been told *ad nauseam* and will not be repeated here. Likewise the tale of the 'River' 2-6-4 tanks, which formed the basis of the 'U' class Moguls; those needing enlightenment are recommended to another tome from this same source, my chapter entitled '2-6-4T' in *In Praise of Steam*. With 'Ns' and 'Us', plus the three-cylinder variants of both, namely the 'N1' and 'U1' classes, Maunsell sired no less than 157 Moguls, a substantial number of locomotives on the smallest of the 'Big Four' Post-Grouping railways, itself spearheading the move into the era of electrification. As with the 'Black Fives' on the LMS, the Maunsell Moguls seemed to attract scant excitement from the railway enthusiasts of the day. Between them they could be found almost anywhere on the Southern during their lifetime, from Kent to Cornwall. Unexciting they may have been, but reliable they most certainly were. It was only the onslaught of dieselisation — a word as ugly as the machine — and electrification that saw them withdrawn.

With Gresley's GNR and LNER 2-6-0s, Churchward's GWR machines and the Maunsell Moguls on the SR, it is both sequential and apposite to turn to the LMS for what was the next major development in this story — a class of locomotive that by its reliability and versatility could arguably be considered the best British Mogul of them all. The 'Crab' probably did more sterling work, for less notice taken, than any single class of steam locomotive. With an exceptionally high running plate and the absence of splashers, the Hughes/Fowler design undoubtedly would have presented a revolutionary appearance at the time of introduction, yet this appearance was incontrovertibly a direct portent of things to come in the world of locomotive design. Although the class appeared after the commencement of the Fowler era on the LMS in 1925, the design was very firmly based on the work of George Hughes, at Horwich, headquarters of the erstwhile Lancashire & Yorkshire Railway (L&Y).

Strangely, the modest amount of literature, and lack of eulogy about the 'Crabs' is mirrored in its parentage. The L&Y is often overshadowed by the Midland and the LNWR when the 'parentage' of the LMS is discussed; and George Hughes himself fades into the background where the foreground is occupied by more glamorous and better-known characters. Yet Hughes was indeed a survivor; 1904-1921 on the L&Y, taking charge when the L&Y

and LNWR merged in 1922, and then becoming first CME of the LMS at the Grouping in 1923. If he had been a politician rather than an engineer, he would probably have been in the Whips' Office!

That the 'Crab' emerged from Horwich in its long-familiar shape and style, and indeed with its excellent boiler, is an example of railway destiny nearly thwarted by fate. In those early years of the LMS, the North Western versus Midland rivalry was bitter, intense and in deadly earnest. J. R. Billinton, mentor on the L&Y of E. S. Cox, and promoted after Grouping to Technical Assistant to the CME George Hughes, died suddenly and unexpectedly in March 1925. By the end of September that year, Hughes had retired to be replaced by Fowler. Thus began, instantaneously, the 'Midland Years' on the LMS. The 'Crab' was well advanced by then but not yet 'on the road'. Only the state of orders placed for parts, and the advanced overall planning, prevented Fowler from inserting a Derby standard boiler on the Mogul. As it was he insisted on the Midland standard 3,500 gallon tender rather than the tender designed by Horwich specifically for the 'Crab'. Thus the 'Crabs' entered, and remained in service, with a tender narrower than the locomotive. Fowler's dictum pertaining to 'things Midland' was similar to that proffered by the late V. T. Saunders, a Master at Uppingham, who tried vainly to teach me something to do, I think, with mathematics; his dreaded weekly classes were called 'Practical Measurement', and to this day his words ring in my head — 'In this classroom there are three ways of doing things: the right way, the wrong way, and my way; and you will do them my way'.

For me, the 'Crabs' were always an exciting sight, although few and far between. Their actual appearance, particularly the chimney, had a distinctly L&Y air. Although they were the first of the LMS mixed-traffic engines, most survived to be withdrawn not through wear and tear, but through the demise of steam. The nickname came from the positioning of the outside cylinders — high up and inclined at a steep angle, and from the working of the outside valve gear.

Notwithstanding their relatively small coupled wheels, they were free-running, and speeds of 75mph were commonplace. They were excellent climbers, but their passenger work was perhaps overshadowed, good indeed as it was, by their tremendous ability for hard-slogging work on heavy freight trains, often on difficult jobs such as the Ayrshire coal hauls; and in atrocious weather they

Below:
Ivatt LMS 2-6-0 No 46411 drifts past Royton Junction with mineral empties, on 22 April 1964. The scene, of industrial Lancashire, causes me pangs of regret that I did not take many more black-and-white photographs: indeed I have a mere handful. No 46411 was for years a Newton Heath engine, surviving there until withdrawal in January 1967. *Author*

Left:
One of the last regular Mogul strongholds was the South Eastern Railway route between Reading, Guildford, Redhill and Tonbridge, where Maunsell's 'N' and 'U' 2-6-0s held sway until the end of steam. That came on 2 January 1965, on which date 'U' No 31799 pulls out of Guildford in charge of the 12.05 Reading (Southern) to Redhill train.

kept their feet. It was the late Derek Cross, on his home territory, who best extracted the photographic potential of these fine machines. So good was the basic design that minor experiments with valve gears on five members of the class of 245 engines were the only attempt to improve a simple, rugged locomotive — and these showed no improvement of the standard Walschaerts valve gear fitted as standard to the class. They provided the fledgling LMS with that railway's first modern standard locomotive, although E. S. Cox, in his inimitable style, states of the 'Crab' that 'its advent at Derby, home of prim inside-cylinder engines and low footplates, was as shocking as that of a striptease girl at a meeting of Plymouth Brethren would have been' (*Locomotive Panorama*).

The 'Crabs' worked freight trains over almost all the LMS system, although perhaps surprisingly they were not used on the Central Wales line. The 'Celtic Fringe' of the LMS system, however, saw some of their finest passenger work, particularly before the introduction of Stanier's 'Black Five'. Not only the Ayr-Stranraer line, but the extremities of the LMS — the Highland line and the Somerset & Dorset — saw them doing fine passenger duty.

A glance at the chart on page 134 may appear to indicate how much more there is to tell, after the 'Crabs', about the development of the British Mogul. Exempting further manifestations of the Maunsell and Gresley designs, which barely rate more than a mention in a superficial study such as this, it is reasonably accurate to state that the 'post-Crab' Mogul story is an 'LMS/BR benefit'. With the arrival of Stanier, the LMS Board hoped, justifiably as it transpired, that the LNWR versus Midland feud, which had so bedevilled locomotive practice on Britain's largest railway, would end. It did. When the operating department requested 40 more mixed-traffic 2-6-0s they anticipated that they would receive more 'Crabs'. They were wrong, as the new CME had other ideas.

Stanier, with his Swindon background, knew what he wanted for the LMS, and it was painfully obvious what the LMS needed — namely more high-powered express engines. What he had in mind was to meld the Swindon style of taper boiler — an unknown quantity at Crewe and Derby — into his new projected Pacific. In order, however, to break new ground gently, Stanier decided to introduce his intentions on the frame of the additionally-required

Moguls. Thus was born the 'Stanier Crab'; although with a higher boiler pressure from the new taper boiler, the wheel diameter was the same as the Hughes-Fowler engines. Contrary to the evidence of a casual glance, they were domeless, but the dome-shaped casing housed the top-feed clacks. The first of the class emerged with the Swindon trademark, the 'milk churn' on top of the boiler — although this feature soon disappeared, on personal instructions from Stanier himself who did not wish to stamp the GWR *imprimatur* of the new LMS engines. Whilst the 'Crabs' acquired their nickname from the angled cylinders, the humped boilers of the Stanier engines inspired the nickname 'Camels' from the Crewe men. Both classes were matched with the Midland tenders, which actually suited the Stanier locomotives better than they suited the 'Crabs'. Both classes, too, gave good service, but were rarely in the public eye in the light of the workaday nature of their tasks.

At the start of this chapter I mentioned the transatlantic links and lineage behind the early British Moguls. The final flowering of the wheel-arrangement on Britain's railways prior to nationalisation also owed much to current American practice. The Ivatt 2-6-0, No 3000, originally classified '4F', emerged from Horwich in 1947, a year after the appearance of the same designer's '2F' (later '2MT') Mogul. The '4F' engine immediately earned itself the *soubriquet* of 'Flying Pig', and thus this chapter's first sentence reveals its source! In Ivatt's own inelegant words, everything had to be 'get-at-able'. The US Transportation Corps' 2-8-0s of Class S160 provided Ivatt with his 'inspiration' if that be the word. With its high running plate, exposed pipework and gross double chimney, the 'Flying Pig' lacked even the grotesque charm of originality of Bulleid's 'Q1'. The smaller Ivatt Mogul was a lot less unattractive, due mainly to a lower running plate, without the gap between it and the top of the cylinder-block. Known as the 'Mickey Mouse' Moguls, the Class 2MTs created a stir for a different reason, namely that their purpose was intended to be that of a modern locomotive for secondary duties, tasks previously, and from time immemorial undertaken by the relegation of the elderly veterans of the motive power department.

Both Ivatt's LMS Moguls survived and prospered through the LMS/BR interregnum: the former were built and utilised under BR auspices as, to all intents and purposes, a BR Standard class, the new BR Standard '4MT' of the '76xxx' class: designed at Doncaster they were less ugly — and thus less distinctive — than the LMS engines. With a wheel diameter of 5ft 3in, 1in bigger, they had slightly inclined cylinders, smaller and less bulky than those of the 'Crab'. No 76114 became the last steam locomotive built at Doncaster, home of the Gresley Moguls. Strangely I do not recall hearing or reading any comment on this design detail. The BR Standard

'2MT' of the '78xxx' class had wheels of 5ft diameter, the same size as the Ivatt 'Mickey Mouse', from which they differed very little indeed, save for a slightly taller and wider chimney and an uncovered top feed. They worked turn and turn about with the Ivatt engines, both types being widely dispersed on the London Midland Region of BR.

Although I have taken the BR Standard Moguls slightly out of chronological order, I have deliberately left until last the 20 engines of Class 3MT — the '77xxx' engines. Unlike the other two BR Moguls, these engines were a new design; but they were virtually superfluous and in retrospect, rather sad. Although none of the four pre-nationalisation companies had bequeathed a Mogul of this size to BR, the fact is that the job for which they were intended was either on cross-country lines, or on trains that, through falling traffic, were light enough to be handled by a Class 2 locomotive. The fact that only 20 emerged from Swindon would indicate that their operational usefulness was recognised as being negligible. Of the total, 10 went to North-East England and 10 to the south of Scotland. Little seems to be written about them, and they appear to have been little-loved. Two photographical memories linger — not of mine, I hasten to add, as I never saw one. One is of two members of the class at the head of a train on the Stainmore Summit line, where one has a rope pulley for uncoupling after banking

duty; and the other is of No 77014 which came down to work an enthusiasts' special on the Southern Region, and stayed there.

The short life-story of No 77014 illustrates the eternal fascination of the steam engine for the besotted enthusiast. In 1957 the 20 members of the

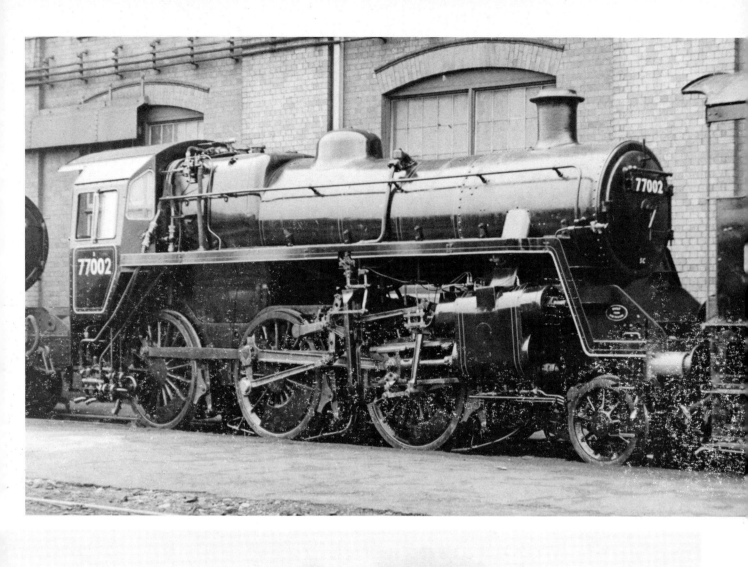

Above:
Some 16 months earlier than the picture of No 31799 on page 140, 'U' 2-6-0 No 31800 heads another Reading to Redhill train, between Wokingham and Crowthorne, on 24 August 1963. Nos 31799 (page 140) and 31800 were amongst the 20 SECR 'River' class 2-6-4 tank engines rebuilt to 2-6-0 tender locomotives following the series of accidents that befell the 'Rivers', culminating in the Sevenoaks accident which led to their withdrawal and rebuilding.

class, as previously mentioned, were scattered about the north of England and south of Scotland, being allocated at this date to Blaydon, Darlington, Hull (Botanic Gardens), West Auckland and Whitby on the erstwhile North-East Region; and to Hamilton, Hurlford and Polmadie on the Scottish Region. In November 1964 Nos 77011/14 were transferred south, to 8E Northwich. As mentioned, No 77014 came down to work that enthusiasts' special, staying on and being officially allocated to 70C Guildford in March 1966. She in fact became the last member of the class to be withdrawn, in July 1967. Whilst none of the class was preserved, No 77014 also became the only member of the class to be scrapped south of the Wash.

Rarely can one wheel-arrangement have completed such a metamorphosis as has the 2-6-0 on Britain's railways. From its inception as a pure freight locomotive, no more than an extended 0-6-0 with a pony-truck, to express and long-distance goods-traffic; through genuine mixed-traffic machines; to perhaps its oddest and certainly its last manifestation, namely the BR Standard Class 3MT of 1954, which seemed to be, if it was anything, a cross-country and secondary passenger locomotive. Indeed 2-6-0 was a versatile wheel-arrangement.

Thanks to the estimable Peter Hands and his painstakingly invaluable series *What Happened to Steam?* one can check on the allocation and withdrawal of literally thousands of individual steam engines from active BR service. Few Moguls lasted into 1968 and the final months of steam. Of the six 'Flying Pigs', all at Lostock Hall Shed, No 43106 was the last survivor, being officially withdrawn on 23 June 1968. I saw and photographed this engine inside Lostock Hall on 4 June 1968. Another member of the class, No 43027, became the subject of my last photograph, of a non-preserved Mogul, at Rose Grove MPD on 31 July 1968. With a 10D Lostock Hall smokebox shedplate, smokebox door ajar, connecting rods removed, she was a sorry sight. Scrapped at Arnott Young's, Dinsdale, the following September, No 43027 went the way of most of the Moguls, from those early Great Eastern machines, through the 'Yankees', 'Krugers', 'Aberdares' and on through the thoroughbreds of Churchward, Gresley, Maunsell. Gone — but not forgotten.

CHAPTER NINE

0-6-0T

Whereas it has been possible in chapters about the 2-6-0 or 4-6-2 to prepare a chart of all the British classes, merely to hint at any such task for the 0-6-0T is enough to make a strong man blanch. Yet without the shunting engine there would have been no railway. One could imagine the GWR without its 'Kings', but without its Panniers — never! Therein perhaps lies the kernel of my task, for it was the numerous, common, workaday, mundane tank engines that oiled the wheels of railway operation.

It is not my intention to try to trace the evolution of the 0-6-0T, arguably because over more than a century it 'evolved' less than any other wheel-arrangement. If one was barely able to include the GWR in the chapter on Pacifics, then no such problem confronts me here; whilst, on the LMS, the '3F' 0-6-0T, known colloquially and to my mind not very attractively as the 'Jinty', also epitomises that railway and its predecessor the Midland Railway. Small wheels, short wheelbase, tall chimney — these were the trademarks of the type. It is numbers, rather than performance or design criteria that set the 0-6-0T apart.

The GWR has many claims to fame. It was the first railway in Britain to use the 4-6-2 wheel-arrangement, and the first to discard it. Whether it was the first to use an 0-6-0T is uncertain. What is clear, however, is that the Great Western built *more* engines of this type than any other railway — not just in Britain, but in the world. From 1860-1956, a total of 2,393 0-6-0Ts was built, of which 1,274 postdated the 1923 Grouping (not that that mattered much on the GWR) and almost all had inside cylinders, the exceptions being the handful in the '1361', '1366' and '15xx' classes. Until the demise of steam brought mass withdrawals, the GWR since 1898 never had less than 1,000 0-6-0Ts in stock. Primarily intended for shunting, they were of course much more widely used, on branch services of all kinds, on freight and local passenger trains, as banking engines and even

on occasion on main line duty when failures occurred and nothing else was to hand. It was the rule rather than the exception that GW Panniers lasted for more than 50 years — many many running mileages approaching the million mark. That they were replaced by diesel shunters is not in dispute; that this was an improvement certainly is.

When considering this wheel-arrangement one cannot omit mention of the distinctive noises made by some of these locomotives. The most memorable for me was the sound of a small GWR tank panting at the platform end, interspersed by what one can only call, in good old Anglo-Saxon language, a rather wet fart. I believe this particular noise was caused by the valve seating of the brake ejector.

Of the 863 members of the '57xx' class of Pannier, I can claim to have rescued one: on 1 March 1986 my colleagues in Commonwealth Holiday Inns of Canada allowed me to have placed on static display No 9629 of the class which, with their consent and the company's money, has been rescued from Dai Woodham's Barry scrapyard, transported to Steamtown at Carnforth, cosmetically fully restored, taken back to Cardiff, displayed there in the GWR 150 Exhibition, and finally put on display outside the Cardiff Holiday Inn. What else but a Great Western Pannier tank could have filled the bill — 'Pannier panache' indeed.

Undoubtedly those Johnson/Fowler '3F' 0-6-0Ts of MR/LMS heritage came nearest to the GW Pannier in distinctive personification of a railway and, a rather poor third, numerically at least, came the North Eastern 'J72'. Of the latter I can write only what I have read, as it was never my good fortune to see one. Of the 'Jinty' there were sights aplenty, and of the Pannier too: sights and sounds, for that marvellous machine was as distinctive to the ear as to the eye. If it is impractical to chart the numerous engines of this wheel-arrangement, let me at least select the three mentioned for my purpose.

145

Details	GWR '57xx'	MR/LMS '3F'	NE/LNER/BR 'J72'
Designer	Collett	Johnson	W. Worsdell
Total number built	863	417	113
First introduced	1929	1924*	1898
Last built	1950		1951
Wheel diameter	4ft 7½in	4ft 7in	4ft 1¼in
Cylinders	17½in×24in	18in×26in	17in×24in
Weight	47tons 10cwt*	49tons 10cwt	38tons 12cwt
Tractive effort	25,515lb	20,835lb	16,760lb
Boiler pressure	200lb/sq in (in SS)	160lb/sq in (in NS)	140lb/sq in (in NS)
Valve gear	Stephenson *Later versions with detail alteration were slightly heavier	Stephenson *Post-Grouping development of Johnson Midland Railway design introduced in 1899	Stephenson

The antecedence of the GWR and MR 0-6-0Ts clearly dates back to the middle of the 19th century, whilst the 'J72' was the last class of the last century to see active service on the North Eastern Region of BR. The original engines, introduced by the North Eastern Railway in 1898, were still being built by the LNER in 1925. Then, astonishingly, a further 28 members of the class, practically unaltered from their Victorian forebears, were built by British Railways between 1949 and 1951. There is no parallel example to be found, certainly in Britain and probably anywhere worldwide, of a design being built at intervals over a period of almost 54 years virtually without design changes.

Withdrawals of the earlier 'J72s' began in 1958; and of the BR-built batch, in 1961. By January 1963 only four remained, all based at Gateshead. In 1964 Nos 69005/23, although officially withdrawn, were transferred to Departmental Stock. No 69005 survived thus until October 1967, and 69023 escaped the cutter's torch, to be preserved.

Having failed to find a class on the Southern, or its constituent companies that, either numerically or in imagery, can claim to fill the role, certainly of the Panniers or 'Jinties', there is nevertheless such a class that holds the affection of innumerable

Below:

This small-wheeled Sharp Stewart 0-6-0ST was built to the drawing dated 16 August 1883. Although the drawing is not in good condition, the attraction of the design outweighs the deterioration of the original document, to earn inclusion in this chapter. What a delightful chimney.

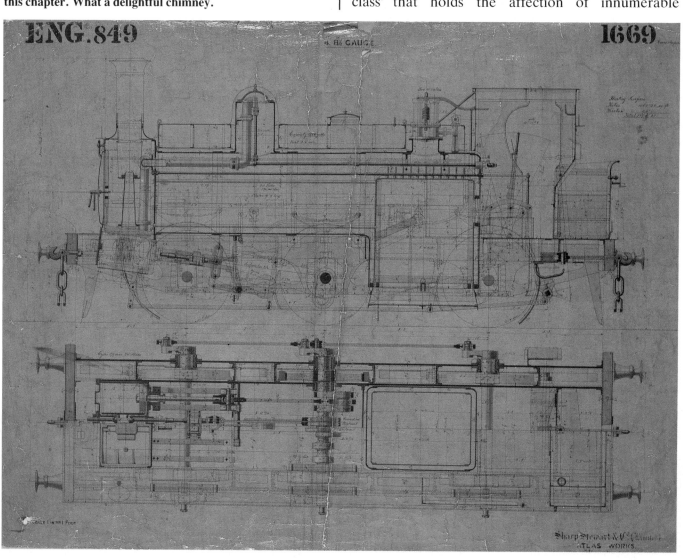

ENG.849

1669

enthusiasts. Albeit not an ubiquitous shunting engine, the Stroudley 'Terriers' could be said to have as many admirers as any other small tank-engine. As ever, Brian Haresnape in his *Stroudley Locomotives*, published in 1985, records immaculately the splendid history of these remarkable engines. Describing the class as '0-6-0T Light Suburban Passenger Tank' he sums up their claim to fame in his opening paragraph thus:

'It is incredible to think that some of a class of small tank engines, designed specifically for South London suburban traffic, and of simple and lightweight construction, should still exist in revenue-earning service, as I write these words, some 111 years later. And yet this is the case with the justly fabled Stroudley "Terriers" — several of which are still used to haul passengers on private preserved railways. This fact becomes all the more remarkable when one discovers that the first LBSCR with-drawals of the class took place in 1901.'

The 'Terriers' were not alone, amongst the very numerous classes and types of 0-6-0T, that were designed for passenger rather than for freight or shunting duties. Few, if any, however were still rostered regularly for scheduled daily passenger service 91 years after their introduction. Brian Haresnape's *Stroudley Locomotives*, records the perhaps surprising information that the only other substantial class of 0-6-0T built by him was the LBSCR Class E and later derivatives. These locomotives, like the majority of 0-6-0T, are described by Brian Haresnape as '0-6-0T Local Goods and Shunting Engines.'

Having mentioned Panniers, the 'J72s' and the 'Terriers', it is to the Midland Railway that one's mind returns as the *eminence grise* of the 0-6-0T. On page 145 I made mention of the Johnson/Fowler '3F' 0-6-0Ts of MR/LMS heritage. That heritage in reality pre-dated Johnson and, operationally, post-

Below:
Tracing a direct lineage between early working drawings of Midland Railway locomotives, and the final manifestation of the London Midland and Scottish Railway 0-6-0 tank engine, the '3F' or 'Jinty', does not require a degree in steam engine anthropology. Here, in the twilight of steam in the area, No 47355 stands on Watford shed on 14 May 1964. Her shedplate has already been stored — or stolen by bounty-hunters.

Above:
Due to the number preserved, and indeed those still working the Havant-Hayling Island service until the line's closure on 4 November 1963, modern and indeed colour photographs abound of Stroudley's 'Terriers'. Here, taken in 1880 in London Brighton & South Coast Railway livery, with contemporary railwaymen, is LBSCR Class A1 0-6-0T No 79 *Minories*. Unlike many of the class to remain in service and indeed in preservation, No 79 was withdrawn in January 1918.

Right:
Prim and pert in the official works photograph from the North Eastern Railway's Darlington Works, and catalogued DAR 813 in the NRM library, is William Worsdell's original 'E1' (and subsequently LNER and BR Class J72) 0-6-0T. It looks like an 1898 creation which makes even more astonishing the BR decision to build an identical new batch of the class from 1949 to 1951. I know of no parallel in Britain of an identical design constructed at intervals over 54 years. Seventy-five were built by the NER between 1898 and 1922; 10 by the LNER at Doncaster in 1925; 28 by BR at Darlington after nationalisation. The class remained intact until 1958 and they were allocated to sheds on the lines of all seven major constituents of the LNER, from King's Cross to Neasden, Wrexham to Ipswich. One only, of the BR batch, No 69023, survived into preservation.

dated Fowler. Although at the date of the Midland Railway livery change from green to red — 1883 — the 110 Johnson 0-6-0 tank-engines were the largest single group of tank engines in service on the MR, it is really to Matthew Kirtley, first Locomotive Engineer of the Midland from 1844 to 1873, that one's mind turns in contemplating the origins of the familiar LMS 0-6-0T. His double-framed locomotives seem to epitomise the strength and durability of Victorian engineering whilst portraying the image of an era of long ago. Kirtley dominated the Midland Railway's locomotive designs, not only for the 30 years that he was in charge, but for years after he had gone to 'the great engine-shed in the sky'. Indeed his wheel-spacing became a tablet of stone on the Midland Railway and into LMS days. William Stanier's 2-6-4 tank engines, and even the great Garratt articulated locomotives, on which none of the criteria which motivated Kirtley could really be relevant, were subjected to the Kirtley wheel-spacing.

Reversion to Kirtley endangers the chronology of this chapter, although its opening sentence high-lighted my difficulty in encompassing a history of so common and numerous a wheel-arrangement in such a superficial manner, in one chapter of one book. Let me draw towards a close, therefore, with passing reference to two classes, one of which I never saw and one of which survived almost to the end of BR steam.

The Great Eastern Railway's Holden 0-6-0 tanks shared perhaps with the Stroudley 'Terriers' the role of the long-lived, essentially passenger locomotive of this wheel-arrangement. To the eyes of railway enthusiasts eking out the final years of British steam, with the electric and dread diesel multiple unit having ousted the intensive steam suburban services in the metropolis many years ago, the sight, sound and smell of the Great Eastern's 'Jazz' trains was one almost too remote to conjure. Liverpool Street station even at the end of the steam era, was a cavernous and gloomy place, with its exit through deprived and depressing inner North-East London's suburbs of the ilk of Bethnal Green and Cambridge Heath — in reality neither 'green' nor 'heath'. Trains that called at these mist-shrouded furtive stations in

Left:
Shades of Southampton docks; in 1983, at Thessaloniki, one of the locomotives of the Greek 'Strategic Reserve' (see page 156) receives attention. The conversion to oil firing has added a new dimension in ugliness to these carbuncular locomotives.

Below:
Ted Richardson was Shedmaster at Feltham at the end of steam; we became firm friends and he would occasionally accompany me to neighbouring sheds. On 23 January 1965, with snow on the ground, we found ourselves at Old Oak Common in its final year of steam, the motive power portending steam's demise in dirt, disinterest and dereliction for those in charge of Western Region. Ted poses beside 'Hall' class 4-6-0 No 5933 *Kingsway Hall*, face to face with '94xx' class 0-6-0PT No 9411. The 'Hall' has lost her nameplate, whilst the Pannier tank is so bereft of fresh paint that the early BR lion-and-wheel emblem has emerged and is clearly visible — as is the power and weight classification, introduced by the GWR in 1920 and denoted by a letter on a coloured disc on the cab side. The latter — in this case D — represents the power classification of the engine, whilst the colour of the circle indicates the routes over which the engine may work. The '94xx' class (as with the '15xx') had a tractive effort of 22,515lb and, with total engine weight of 55.3 tons these locomotives had a restricted route availability, to the aggravation of the Running Superintendent.

Above:
**The Ian Allan *Locomotive and Locoshed Book* tells the tale
through its prosaic headings. '0-6-0T. 2F. Class J72.
Introduced 1898. W. Worsdell N.E. design.' The numerical
gap commences after 68754, and here we see the first of the
BR-built batch, as detailed on page 146.**

Right:
**Remarks related to Johnson Midland 0-6-0s apply with equal
facility to the GWR '57xx' 0-6-0 Pannier tanks: endless
photographs of numerous locomotives with a variety of minor
alterations. Maurice Earley captures the jauntiness, three
years after Nationalisation, of one of the class still bearing
GWR lettering. No 5766 leaves Henley-on-Thames in 1951
with the auto-train for Twyford.**

the first decade of this century, with city clerks and
typists en route to Enfield and Chingford, would not
want to linger in the gathering dusk. Pert engines
with tiny cylinders, small wheels and stove-pipe
chimneys brought their suburban stock in, paused
and were off briskly before anything untoward
occurred. With driving wheels of a mere 4ft nothing,
yet immaculate in Royal Blue, these engines must
surely have been as distinctive a hallmark of their
generation, and indeed of the steam era, as any of
the grand machines that fill the pages of nostalgic
reminiscence — the 'Kings', or the Gresley, Stanier
and Bulleid Pacifics. Although, unlike the more
famous and fashionable 'Terriers', the Holden GER
0-6-0 tanks were, in fact, originally intended for
shunting and trip-freight duties when first introduced
in 1886, they were modified with raised boiler
pressure and Westinghouse brake and adopted as the
Great Eastern's standard suburban passenger class.
The original engines and the later ones had cast-iron
wheels, but following their adoption as the suburban
tank, a large batch was built with cast steel wheels.

Above:
'USA' 0-6-0T No 30072 was built by Vulcan Ironworks at Wilks-Barre, Pennsylvania in 1943, shipped to Britain, acquired by the Southern Railway and then subsequently by BR. She finished her BR days as Guildford shed pilot where I photographed her on 25 May 1963. Happily this engine is one of those to have survived into preservation and is now on the Keighley & Worth Valley Railway.

Below:
Only 10 '15xx' class Pannier tanks were built. With 4ft 7½in driving wheels, these stocky, compact engines, classified '4F', were a far cry mechanically from the early Wolverhampton and Swindon locomotives of this type, but as with the MR/LMS 0-6-0 tank engines, the visual lineage was clear. A shaft of sunlight pierces the grime of Old Oak Common's roof to illuminate No 1503 on 23 June 1963.

The Holden 0-6-0Ts subsequently classified 'J67' and 'J69' by the LNER, were perpetuated by his successor as Locomotive Superintendent on the Great Eastern, A. J. Hill, himself the originator of the 0-6-2T subsequently to monopolise LNER suburban work: but that is another story. The final 10 of these distinctive little 0-6-0 tanks were built in 1912, under Hill's stewardship, with copper-capped chimneys in place of the GE 'stovepipe' on the Holden engines. As mentioned earlier, they must have been a sight for sore eyes. Wide indeed is the gap between the glory of gleaming Pre-Grouping colour, and the invention and availability of colour film: although the passage of time doubtless heightens the glamour, embellishes the memory and titillates the imagination. There were doubtless dirty engines before 1923.

From unseen but imagined glory, to well-remembered mundanity would seem appropriate as this chapter and indeed this book approach their close. The last totally new class of 0-6-0T to make its appearance on the tracks of a British railway was ugly, alien and in its day aesthetically unloved. Only the passage of time and the demise of steam could generate affection for those USA tanks. Imported into Britain during the second world war, 14 of these locomotives, introduced in 1942, were purchased by the Southern Railway in 1946, having been fitted with modified cab and bunker, as well as other detail alterations. Notwithstanding their unsympathetic physical appearance — no mistaking these for a Maunsell design — they earned a good reputation amongst those who worked on and with them. Southampton Docks was, with the exception of No 30063, their stamping ground until the arrival of the diesels at the end of 1962, when the members of the class were dispersed, to Departmental Stock, to Eastleigh, and one to Guildford. Unlike their larger American predecessors, the 'S160' 2-8-0s, the USA tanks made no contribution to British locomotive design ideas. One, No 30072, was latterly shed pilot at Guildford MPD and is now preserved on the Keighley and Worth Valley Railway. I saw No 30072 on shed pilot duty at Guildford on the last weekend of steam on the Reading-Redhill line, on 2 January 1965; but unusually my first sighting of one of these machines was not on shed or in service, but rusting on the scrapline at Eastleigh, where I photographed No 30070 on 18 May 1963. My last photograph of a 'USA' 0-6-0T, however, was not in Britain, but at Thessaloniki in Greece in September 1983. There were quite a few rotting away in the locomotive dumps in that city, overgrown, but still easily identifiable. However, two members of the class, converted for oil-firing, were on shed, in good condition and, so I was told, part of the Greek Strategic Reserve. When I enquired as to the nature of the emergency for which these locomotives were

Below:
LMS '3F' 0-6-0T No 47480, one of the few push-pull fitted members of the class, stands at the entrance to Newton Heath shed, with the carriage works in the background, on 3 December 1964. *Author*

kept in running order, I was told that it was a precaution against an oil crisis that might strangle the Greek railways diesel locomotives. My next question, however, seemed to drop like a bombshell, and had seemingly not been asked before: 'What is the point of keeping oil-fired steam engines as part of a strategic reserve in the event of an oil crisis . . .?'

Before finally leaving the subject of American-built 0-6-0 tank engines imported into the UK in time of war, my attention has been drawn whilst preparing this book, to another earlier 0-6-0T, built by Baldwin for the War Department — ours not theirs. I knew nothing of these machines until

research for this book caused me to contact the Smithsonian Institution in Washington. They aimed me in the direction of Mr Herb Broadbelt of Newport News, Virginia, the owner of the copyright of large numbers of old Baldwin Locomotive Works photographs. On receipt of Mr Broadbelt's catalogue, my eye was caught by entry No 6686, which was thus described: 'British Government: Loco and Views: 0-6-0 1917'. Thus I obtained a photograph of what might be described as the grandfather of the 1942 'USA' 0-6-0 tanks. (See below.)

I digress. Lest anyone should seek to disagree with my statement on page 156, that the USA 0-6-0T was

Above:
This Baldwin locomotive is described on the photograph supplied by Herb Broadbelt, as '0-6-0 1917 built for British Government (War Department)'. That it is an 0-6-0T is self-evident. The manufacturers' plate on the side of the smokebox embellishes this scanty information only with the addition of works number 46673 and the precise date of October 1917.

Left:
In November 1985, on the East Somerset Railway, LMS '3F' 0-6-0T No 47493, suitably adorned with 82H shedplate, gives a good appearance of timelessness. Thanks to David Shepherd, HTV and a foul wet day, one got quite near to the 'real thing' on this most delightful of all preserved railways.

the last 'totally new' class of this wheel-arrangement
to appear on our railway system, I should doubtless
mention the final flowering of the Great Western
0-6-0 Pannier Tanks of Classes 15xx, 16xx and 94xx.
All were Hawksworth's designs, and indeed the first
two classes appeared only after the GWR had
(officially) ceased to exist on the nationalisation of
Britain's railways.

The '94xx' Panniers, of which 210 were built, were
reputedly a product of the (shall we call it) 'vanity' of
the GWR Directors. More Panniers were needed in
1947, but the Board apparently felt that the large
dome on the '57xx' class was too ancient-looking to
be seen on Paddington empty stock duty, notwithstanding the excellence and versatility of the 853
members of the class in service. Thus Hawksworth

produced his domeless large '94xx', the first 10 of
which were built at Swindon in 1947. Perhaps my
comment that this was not a really 'new' design,
made in relation to the appearance of the USA
tanks, should be modified in that the locomotive
combined for the first time two of the GWR's most
distinctive features — the pannier tank and the taper
boiler.

There was nothing mechanically wrong with these
locomotives, other than that their extra size and
weight gave them a more restricted route availability
than the '57xx', (see photograph on page 151), and
initially presented drivers with a problem due to
their inability to reach the brake valve when leaning
out of the cab — not an advantage when shunting.
This was soon rectified, and following nationalisation
and the changes made to certain regional bound-
aries, a number of '94xx' Panniers went to
Bromsgrove to undertake Lickey banking duties.
Thus after perhaps the GWR's greatest failure,
namely the loss to the Midland Railway of the
acquisition of the Birmingham & Gloucester
Railway in 1845, Great Western locomotives finally
obtained a base on the line.

Of the two other classes, namely the '15xx' and
'16xx', built after nationalisation, the '15xx' did bring
one substantial change to standard GWR practice,
namely the provision of outside cylinders and

Above:
Personification of the wheel-arrangement, and of the railway which itself was personified by the 0-6-0 tank engine; GWR '57xx' Pannier tank No 7708 bisects gantries of semaphore signals on a trip freight at Reading in December 1953. With 863 engines, the '57xx' class was numerically the largest in the country. Variations included design of cab, and a few had, variously, condensing apparatus for working through the Metropolitan line tunnels, and steam brakes only for those members of the class, mainly in South Wales, whose duties were restricted to shunting.

Walschaerts valve-gear, although the class — of which only 10 were built — was a development of the '94xx' having the same boiler. These locomotives had a very short wheelbase and were specifically designed for heavy shunting duties. They were, sadly, an anachronism in the light of the BR policy of proliferating the diesel shunter, although argument continues to this day as to the respective merits of the alternative forms of motive power. The '15xx' class represent, possibly the most grotesque example of financial waste, being sacrificed almost as soon as they were 'run in', on the altar of modernisation.

Final mention, then, falls to the '16xx' class of Pannier. Whereas the '15xx' were classified by BR as '4F', the small '16xx' were rated as '2F'. They were pert little locomotives visibly Great Western, although two were transferred almost as far as it was possible to travel from GW metals — to the Highland Railway's Dornoch branch. A total of 70 of these engines was built between 1949 and 1955, and they can certainly claim to be the last 0-6-0 tanks to be built for Britain's railways.

The 0-6-0 tank engine lasted almost to the end of steam; surely the longest-lasting wheel-arrangement on Britain's railways. Appropriately to end this chapter, my last photographs, in 1966, of 0-6-0 tanks, were of a GWR Pannier tank, and an LMS '3F' — both clearly reminiscent of their Pre-Grouping forebears from Great Western and Midland Railways. Continuity, a sense of history and loyalty; these indeed were the hallmarks of the steam engine, and its dominant and irreplaceable role in the life of and affection for Britain's railways.

INDEX

A comprehensive index is not included: this is an index only to the photographs within the book, catalogued alphabetically under the name of the railway which built and/or operated the relevant locomotive class or wheel-arrangement. Pre-Grouping classes are referred to by their latterly-known nomenclature, arbitrarily decided by the author in the hope of achieving convenience for the reader.